LISA DELLMUTH

WITH A FOREWORD
BY BO ROTHSTEIN

IS EUROPE GOOD FOR YOU?

EU Spending and Well-Being

BRISTOL
UNIVERSITY
PRESS

First published in Great Britain in 2021 by

Bristol University Press
University of Bristol
1-9 Old Park Hill
Bristol
BS2 8BB
UK
t: +44 (0)117 954 5940
e: bup-info@bristol.ac.uk

Details of international sales and distribution partners are available at
bristoluniversitypress.co.uk

British Library Cataloguing in Publication Data
A catalogue record for this book is available from the British Library

ISBN 978-1-5292-1746-9 hardcover
ISBN 978-1-5292-1747-6 ePub
ISBN 978-1-5292-1748-3 ePdf

Cover design: Clifford Hayes
Image credit: Rainbow circle formed by men, women, boys and girls holding hands © PeterHermesFurian.

Printed and bound by CPI Group (UK) Ltd, Croydon, CR0 4YY

MIX
Paper | Supporting responsible forestry
FSC® C013604

Contents

List of Figures and Tables

Figures

Tables

Acknowledgements

This book is the product of many discussions and a great deal of collaborative thinking. My deepest gratitude is to Hans Agné, for brilliant ideas about how to connect theories of well-being and distributive justice; to Erik Hegelund, who generously shared his knowledge of econometrics in the study of unemployment; to Dominik Schraff, who offered astute comments that led me to consider the implications of this book for democratic legitimacy; and to Jonas Tallberg, for incisive comments and consistent support for this project.

Ognjen Zugic and I spent many hours together discussing data analysis and interpretation, and the statistical components of my argument are substantially inspired by those meetings. Ogi contributed significantly to the statistical analysis and deftly drafted parts of what later became Chapter Four and Chapter Five, each of which was made stronger as a result.

This study has also benefited from discussions in seminars at the Department of Economic History and International Relations at Stockholm University. Many thanks to those with whom I have discussed various aspects of this work: Lars Ahnland, Tanja Dannwolf, Susanne Dellmuth, Rodney Edvinsson, Maria-Therese Gustafsson, Liesbet Hooghe, Judith Kelley, Björn Ljung, Christian Rauh, Jan Aart Scholte and Karina Shyrokykh. I am also grateful to Lisa Cardyn and Andrew Mash for candid and insightful language advice. I would also like to thank Elisa Funk, Agnese Loy and Ana-Sofia Valderas for their excellent research assistance. This project was generously funded by the Early Career Grant awarded by the Regional Studies Association (RSA) in 2015. The staff of the RSA deserves special recognition for the exceptional courtesy and encouragement they provided as I pursued my work.

My thanks also go to the 189 government officials at subnational and national levels in Germany, Greece and the UK, and in multiple institutions within the European Union (EU), who either spoke with me anonymously or completed an online survey on EU regional policy. Together, these participants have significantly enhanced my understanding of the politics of EU regional development funding and its effects on Europe's regions.

Finally, I am endlessly indebted to my family: Susanne, Paul, Björn, Stellan, Tulle, Ingrid, Staffan, and Shae. This book is dedicated to my beloved children.

Foreword

Bo Rothstein
August Röhss Chair in Political Science
University of Gothenburg

Issues about social and economic inequality have received increased attention lately. One example of this is that four major international economic policy organizations that historically did not care much about inequality – the Organisation for Economic Co-operation and Development (OECD), the World Economic Forum, the World Bank and the International Monetary Fund (IMF) – now are issuing warnings that the current level of economic inequality in developed countries is not socially sustainable. Since the 1980s, economic inequality has sky-rocketed in most OECD countries. One example is Sweden, which used to be a showcase for the possibility of combining a successful market economy with a low level of poverty. During the last two decades, the country has seen one of the most dramatic increases in economic inequality. In this important book, Lisa Dellmuth shows that Europe has experienced a poverty and economic inequality standstill in both rich and poor subnational regions since the 1990s. The central question asked is if the EU's ambition to support regional social and economic development has served as an instrument against this increased economic inequality by, for example, supporting employment possibilities, quality education and improved population health for disadvantaged citizens.

An important result from this study is that social investments launched by the EU so far have had only weak effects on well-being in rich regions and adverse effects on well-being in poor regions. A key empirical finding is that EU social investments have exacerbated income inequality in poor regions, as the spending mostly benefits already wealthy groups in these regions. Political promises for a more 'inclusive growth' or making the EU a 'social investment state' have not been fulfilled. Since the EU faces a declining confidence from its citizens and severe problems concerning political legitimacy, this massive policy failure needs to be addressed. Much of the debate about legitimacy problems for the EU has focused on the issue of a 'democratic deficit'. Citizens cannot make their voices heard because of the complicated system for political representation in the EU. However, research in political science shows that when citizens make up their mind as to whether they perceive their government to be legitimate, what takes place on the 'output' side of the political system is often more important for them than issues about political representation at the 'input' side. Both *what* they get in terms of policies that support their life situation and also *how* they are treated by government institutions that implement such policies turn out to be very significant factors for government legitimacy growth.

This book raises a key question relevant for these debates, namely, how the EU ought to complement domestic welfare states through social investments. The author puts forward a convincing argument that the EU can and should use social investments to enhance regional well-being, defined as a condition of distributive justice in a region through which poor and otherwise vulnerable people are provided with the capabilities to achieve a good quality of life. The theory draws from political philosophy and welfare economics, especially the theory of capabilities by Nobel laureate Amartya Sen. This book should be seen as an evidence base for a debate among practitioners, scientists, and perhaps even the broader public on how the EU can use spending to implement policies that can alleviate poverty in poor regions and promote well-being for all Europeans. In short, how the EU can change what has become known as 'inclusive growth' from a mere political slogan to a de facto implemented policy.

Preface

My interest in what the EU can do to promote well-being within its borders was ignited in the aftermath of the global financial crisis of 2007–12. Much of the public debate at the time focused on structural reforms, public spending and government liabilities, but there was strikingly little emphasis on Europeans' standard of living. The effects of so severe an economic downturn were felt not only by the young, the poor and the low-skilled, to name just a few vulnerable groups, but also by wider segments of society. A number of leading political thinkers, economists and organizations urged us to recognize the importance of well-being in developed societies in publications such as *The Stiglitz Report* (2010); *How's Life?*, a biennial report by the OECD, which was first published in 2011; and the United Nations (UN) Sustainable Development Goal 3, 'Ensure healthy lives and promote well-being for all at all ages'. In the light of the current economic downturn linked to the COVID-19 pandemic, it is even more important to think about how to alleviate the differences in well-being in European society.

It is possible that the enduring social impact of the 2007–12 crisis and the current downturn among the public-at-large will be limited to pessimism and uncertainty about the future, as well as growing frustration with national and European politicians. There may also be an opportunity, however, to recast the regional inequalities that deeply affect citizens' lives and the unfair distribution of income, and also to rethink what the EU can do about these. Can EU regional development funding be allocated and deployed in a manner that supports many people's quest for suitable employment or a good education? Can it help to improve public health and enhance the skills of poor and otherwise disadvantaged people so they are able to command higher wages? Can it brighten young people's education and employment prospects? Will it be possible to use EU funding to promote a more just income distribution?

In the EU, achieving improved regional well-being, defined as enhanced distributive justice and strengthened individual capabilities, is a persistent policy challenge that, especially since 2000, it has sought to meet through social investment as part of its European Structural and Investment Funds. A key finding of this book is that these social investments have positive but modest effects on labour market outcomes in rich regions, but no effects at all on youth activity levels, public health, poverty or income inequality. At the same time, EU social investments are found to have contributed to exacerbating income inequality in poor regions.

This book provides firm evidence that EU social investments benefit the already wealthy and makes the case for a rethink on regional inequality. It also discusses the implications for wider debates about inclusive growth and legitimacy across the EU. In light of the debate about growing nationalist populism in the EU, these issues have seen renewed interest in recent years. The book is written for practitioners, students and specialists in political science, economics and related disciplines. The mathematical equations and methodological discussions have been moved to the appendix of this book. Readers will also find a supplementary online appendix on the book's homepage (https://bristoluniversitypress.co.uk/is-europe-good-for-you) with more detailed information on the data as well as additional analyses that underline the robustness of the results.

Those prone to take a rigid stance on the prospects for EU regional policy will not find much comfort within the pages of this book. Instead, this book aims to provide a scientific foundation for open and constructive dialogue on how spending rules and practices in the EU need changing to improve regional well-being.

In short, the socio-economic divide writ large is about more than comparative rates of income. Household income inequality is a symptom of unequal opportunities to obtain an education, participate in social activities, access high-quality jobs, maintain good health and earn an adequate income (OECD, 2017a, 2017b). The notion of well-being goes beyond gross domestic product (GDP) to understanding citizens' real-world options.

The 2019–20 global coronavirus pandemic (COVID-19) and the resulting global economic downturn has fuelled the debate about well-being and inclusive growth. Like the 2007–12 crisis, we are now witnessing a surge in public debt that could lead to severe cuts in social investments (or 'social spending') and thus have serious repercussions for well-being. The fiscal situation in the EU member states varied greatly before the 2007–12 crisis, but those states with higher levels of public debt and less economic power, such as Ireland and the southern European economies, were forced to make deeper cuts in social spending in the aftermath of the crisis. Economic adjustment programmes agreed by the 'Troika' of the European Commission, the European Central Bank and the IMF required a significant curtailment of public spending and the social security system. Several states took this approach, typically in an attempt to comply with the EU's debt rules (Cylus and Pearson, 2015). More recently, country indicators from 2018 suggest that life is getting better in the EU in terms of labour market outcomes, but that poverty and income inequality are persistent problems that have remained largely similar across rich and poor states (OECD, 2020a).

Prompted by the ongoing debate about the transformation of traditional welfare states into active – and 'retrenched' – social investment states, this book puts the concept of well-being front and centre. Beckfield (2019) has underlined the importance of rigorous analyses of the effects of European integration on welfare states and inequality regimes. Busemeyer (2014) has made the case for considering inequalities, institutions and public attitudes together in a single equation in order to better understand the trajectories of welfare states. Piketty (2014) has called for a greater appreciation of the distribution of wealth in economic theory, and welfare economists have repeatedly emphasized well-being as an important variable for measuring socio-economic development alongside GDP, not least to encourage political thinking about inclusive growth (Fitoussi et al, 2010; Son, 2011; Stiglitz et al, 2018).

The European Structural and Investment Funds, which at about €45 billion per year account for more than a third of the EU budget, are the EU's main instrument to promote inclusive growth.[3] These funds undergird an EU regional policy that seeks to promote 'social and economic cohesion' by part-financing domestic social and economic investment. Cohesion is firmly associated with regional performance and has traditionally been understood as GDP differences between regions. Since the 2000s, however, our understanding of cohesion has changed to now include both economic development and social justice within regions as two central goals of EU spending (Begg, 2003; Begg and Bachtler, 2017). In the words of Begg (2009, p. 12), this shift in the understanding of cohesion has put the question of how to resolve 'the balance between "pure" competitiveness-enhancing investments and "pure" solidarity transfers' centre stage.

A large body of economics scholarship has studied the effects of EU spending on economic convergence between regions. A central insight is that EU funding has positive effects on economic growth, especially in a few highly competitive regions (Bouvet, 2010; Farole et al, 2011; Mohl, 2016). However, we know little about the effects of EU spending on one of the crucial outcomes: differences in well-being between citizens within regions. EU spending effects on well-being have yet to be systematically examined.

To enable such an analysis, I have sought to take account of the effects of EU spending on improving regional circumstances that are crucial to shaping individual choices and opportunities has clear limits. GDP does not take account of the distribution of well-being across the population (Amin and Tomaney, 1995, p. 13; Mahler and Ramos, 2019). It also ignores the many other social and economic changes that individuals may experience and that, in the aggregate, shape collective regional well-being (Fitoussi et al, 2010; Adler and Fleurbaey, 2016). Nonetheless, the previous literature on regional inequalities typically continued to use GDP as an indicator of regional welfare (Heidenreich and Wunder, 2008; Bouvet, 2010). Two notable exceptions are isolated studies on the determinants of intra-regional employment (Mohl, 2016) and income inequality (Castells-Quintana et al, 2015).

Most of the debate about the effects of EU spending on growth has been preoccupied with the effects of domestic institutions and factor endowment. Firmly anchored in macroeconomics, the factor of production most responsible for fostering a growth effect from EU spending is widely held to be human capital. It is also seen as a proxy indicator of the absorptive capacity of a region. It is skills that will shape the linkage between EU funding and growth, and there must be a minimum average skill level in a regional economy to enable that region to absorb or use EU funds effectively (Bähr, 2008). Moreover, the positive effects of EU funding on growth are shown to increase with the quality of government institutions and decline with the level of corruption – and high-quality governance and low levels of corruption are the hallmarks of Europe's richer regions (Ederveen et al, 2006; see also Charron et al, 2013).

These EU findings dovetail well with macro-economic theories that suggest that human capital (Becker et al, 2011) and quality of government (Acemoglu et al, 2005) are central determinants of the development and adoption of new technology, both of which are pro-growth factors. These findings are also in line with broader theories in development economics, which suggest that international development aid – such as the funds provided by the World Bank – is put to more productive use when absorptive capacity in the recipient country is high (Burnside and Dollar, 2000).

Technological development also has a central place in the debate. Based on insights from 'new growth theory', technological advancement crucially depends on investment in education, and research and development (Romer, 1994). From this vantage point, high-quality intra-regional government makes it more likely that new technologies will be made available, especially in less economically developed regions. In turn, technological opportunities can facilitate a structural transition from an agricultural regional economy to an industrial one (Fagerberg and Verspagen, 1996) and increase the likelihood that EU funds will be efficiently absorbed (Becker et al, 2012). However, technologies are not public goods. Technology gap theory contends that innovation will be unequally distributed across regions, stimulating economic growth and slowing economic convergence in some regions, but not in others (Fagerberg, 1987). Growth-inhibiting technology gaps can be exacerbated by a heavy reliance on agriculture (Fagerberg and Verspagen, 1996) and by high levels of regional unemployment. The higher the rate of unemployment, the lower the inflows of risk capital and the number of qualified prospective employees, which in turn will increase the outflow of investment (Fagerberg et al, 1997) and the level of skills depreciation in the workforce (Cappelen et al, 2003) – all of which are growth-impeding factors.

It is known that most of the economic growth over the past 30 years occurred in a relatively small number of highly competitive regions, underlining the mixed usefulness of EU funding for growth (Heidenreich and Wunder, 2008; Farole et al, 2011; Beckfield, 2019). Inspired by this puzzle, several political-economic studies have attempted to explain the allocation of EU regional funds. GDP is clearly the most powerful determinant of how EU funds are allocated, but there is also evidence that electoral politics can distort needs-based allocations (Kemmerling and Bodenstein, 2006; Bouvet and

Dall'erba, 2010; Dellmuth and Stoffel, 2012; Chalmers, 2013; Schraff, 2014; Dellmuth et al, 2017). Such distortions should be minor, however, and therefore not severely undermine EU spending effects, given that EU fund allocations remain mostly needs-based. In addition, while there is evidence that EU funds tend to crowd out national investment in regions (Mohl, 2016), this dynamic has been shown to be behind only a fraction of the decline in public investment (Alegre, 2012).

Taken together, the literature is rich in evidence on growth effects of EU funding but does not systematically study well-being effects. What is more, EU rules and their incentives for regional and national governments who devise regional investment strategies together with the Commission and select investment projects, and the resulting consequences for the socio-economic effects of EU spending, remain understudied.

The argument

Examining the linkages between EU funds and GDP growth is important but provides an insufficient understanding of regional development. Unless opportunities are provided to enhance well-being, enormous human potential will continue to be lost. A focus on well-being has the distinct advantage of being complex and multifaceted and providing a wide-angle perspective on the socio-economic problems that confront the EU. Regional well-being encompasses a number of vital aspects of human life, such as patterns and levels of employment, good health, income and social inclusion. Foregrounding this concept provides a clearer window on the larger picture that can be measured and empirically studied (see also Stiglitz et al, 2018), allowing for nuanced analysis of key components of the regional context in which social and economic life occurs.

Specifically, I propose to use the concept of *regional well-being* to capture regional inequalities. Chapter Three defines regional well-being as a condition of distributive justice in a region through which poor and otherwise vulnerable people are provided with the capabilities to achieve a good quality of life. I write in the tradition of welfare economics and well-being research that focuses on objective well-being as a standard of living or a set of individual achievements (for example, Rawls, 1971; Sen, 1985; Son, 2011; Stiglitz et al, 2018). This approach pertains to a long line of reflection going back to Aristotle, John Stuart Mill and John Hicks, among others, that argues that well-being should be conceived in terms of functionings and capabilities, instead of resources (Alkire, 2016). The reason is that a focus on resources excludes consideration of the variability in individuals' actual capabilities to convert resources into valuable outcomes (Sen, 1985, p. 200). *Capability* refers to the real opportunity that we have to accomplish what we value; *functionings* are beings and doings that people value and have good reasons to value.

This approach to well-being places this book squarely in the tradition of theories of 'objective well-being', which are concerned with how an individual's circumstances promote their well-being, as opposed to 'subjective well-being' theories, which foreground the individual's personal experience of well-being and typically define well-being as happiness and life satisfaction.

To the notion of regional well-being as distributive justice, I add those of social and economic investment. The distinction between social and economic funding is central to the arguments in this book. Economic funds seek to improve competition in the context of increasing Europeanization and market globalization, mainly through capital subsidies to business, energy, food, healthcare and transport infrastructure – or, in other words, 'efficiency'. By contrast, social funds correspond to 'social investments' intended to support citizens throughout their life course, mainly through investments in education and skills – and thus promote equity. While efficiency is about reductions in *inter*-regional disparities in welfare, equity is about diminishing *intra*-regional disparities. Using this distinction,

I argue that EU spending will enhance regional well-being if appropriate reforms are undertaken to maintain and expand social investments in the capabilities and skills of the poorest and most vulnerable.

To cut straight to the heart of the matter, under the current legal framework domestic social investment practices using EU funds will continue to benefit already highly skilled and wealthy regions and groups. As I show in this book, especially since 2000 EU regional policy has claimed to regard the fight against poverty and social exclusion as paramount in the determination of spending targets. EU spending seeks to advance domestic investment in growth and active labour market policies, as well as tackling poverty and social inclusion – all of which are highly relevant to many of the underlying processes associated with inequality.

Thus, EU regional policy has been influenced by a broader trend in intellectual and political thinking about how to transform existing passive welfare states into social investment states. The ability of nation states to create equal societies using traditional approaches that combine growth-enhancing investments with palliative social welfare policies has been increasingly questioned over the past 20 years (Esping-Andersen, 2002; Hemerijck, 2013). The basic idea behind the social investment state is that social investments rather than passive social transfers could be the key to modernizing European welfare states. From this vantage point, investing in citizens' skills rather than compensating them after the event for income and job losses could increase the prospects of empowering individuals while also contributing to economic growth (Morel et al, 2012; Busemeyer et al, 2018).

While EU regional funding has long been based on a belief that reducing *inter*-regional disparities should be the end goal (Rumford, 2000), the social goal of investing in lifelong education and building human capital to alleviate poverty and inequalities in the form of *intra*-regional disparities has become increasingly mainstream in the regulatory framework governing

EU regional funding. Since 2000 in particular, the EU has emphasized social goals in its employment policies (Scharpf, 2002; de la Porte and Natali, 2018), and social investments are now an integral part of EU regional spending policies (Chapter Two).

Given that the EU budget is very small compared to domestic budgets and has never exceeded 1 per cent of EU GDP, why does any of this matter? Consider that government spending in a typical Western European economy is equivalent to about 50 per cent of GDP (IMF, 2021). There are three main reasons. First, a conditionality attached to the EU funds requires domestic public or private sector co-funding. In poorer regions, co-funding rates are typically around 20 per cent of the EU funds received, while in richer regions this rises to about 50 per cent. Thus, EU funding promotes additional domestic spending beyond existing programmes and has an important steering function.

Second, for many citizens, EU regional funds have become tangible resources, which means that the EU can take credit for the funding. Around 30–45 per cent of citizens across all EU member states are aware of the EU support provided to their city or region. This is a considerable proportion and reflects a more general trend of growing public awareness of and debate about EU institutions and policies (Hooghe and Marks, 2009; de Wilde and Zürn, 2012). Flash Eurobarometer (FEB) polls from 2008, 2010, 2013 and 2015 suggest that, on balance, citizens are aware of 'EU regional policy' and 'EU co-financed projects'. More than one third of respondents indicated some knowledge of these policies in a given year. These polls also show a consistent link between awareness of the spending measures and receipt of funding. For instance, awareness tends to be much higher among individuals living in regions 'that have been eligible for funds in previous years' (FEB, 2008) or are 'eligible for support under the Convergence objective' (FEB, 2010, 2013, 2015), which constitutes a majority of EU funding.

Third, several features of the institutional environment in the EU multilevel polity prevent EU funds from benefiting the poor and otherwise disadvantaged. Part of the problem is that the amount of social spending has historically been low. Figure 1.1 illustrates that most EU regional funding – about 70 per cent – is in the form of economic funding or capital subsidies rather than social funding or investment in human capital. For the purposes of this book, I have coded these two types of funding according to how the funding targets are labelled in the information contained in the spreadsheets provided by the Commission's Directorate-General for Regional and Urban Policy (DG Regio) and the annual reports on the structural funds. For example, the purchase of capital goods or the construction of warehouses is economic funding, whereas financial support for vocational training programmes or civil society projects linked to labour market integration and migrants constitutes social funding (see Appendix B). Social funding is mostly but not exclusively allocated through the ESF.[4]

Figure 1.1 shows that social investments in people's skills and abilities to escape poverty and social exclusion have declined since 2008, while economic investments have been rising. Since then, intra-regional well-being problems have increased and levels of inequality have risen, in richer regions in particular. Economic investments made have steadily increased in real terms since 1995, but social funds stopped increasing in 2007 and then began to decline. This is true of both overall spending shown on the left and spending in relation to national economic activity in terms of GDP shown on the right. All the EU member states apart from the Czech Republic and Germany experienced a decrease in EU social investment receipts in the period 2007–13, in part due to capacity problems to absorb all earmarked EU funds. Interestingly, domestic social spending did not compensate for this decline, as many member states also cut their social spending after the crisis (OECD, 2020b). As EU spending

Figure 1.1: EU regional economic and social funding

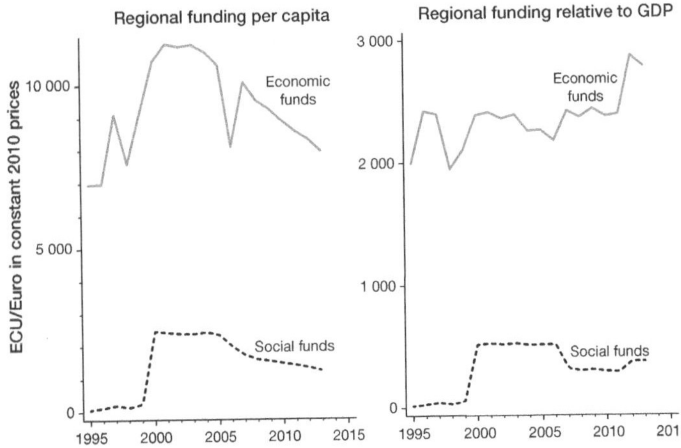

Notes: Inflation-adjusted payment data in constant 2010 prices. Inductive coding of spending data (see Appendix B).

co-funds and therefore influences domestic investment, a declining amount of EU social investment can be expected to have an effect on well-being.

Crucially, EU social spending has remained at less than one fifth of total EU regional spending since the beginning of the 1990s. It is true that lifelong learning has been emphasized as an explicit goal since 2000 and funded through the European Structural and Investment Funds. In addition, under the current 2014–20 multiannual financial framework (MFF), €31.3 billion has been earmarked to invest in lifelong learning and about €20.4 billion is set aside for promoting social inclusion and poverty reduction, especially by improving public services. However, these amounts are just 10 and 6 per cent of the European Structural and Investment Funds, respectively.[5] Chapter Two shows how the budgetary framework for 2014–20 led to social policy initiatives such as the European Pillar of Social Rights, which drove social investments to combat inequalities of opportunity, skills gaps and poverty (de la

Porte and Natali, 2018), but that, even so, social spending has stubbornly remained at about one fifth of the total regional funds budget for the past 25 years.

In terms of governance, regional and national governments are responsible for drawing up regional multiannual funding plans and selecting social investment projects in line with the EU's social goals. Social goals are mainstreamed into the regulatory framework but are undermined during domestic fund implementation. The EU's institutional framework does not provide enough incentives to nudge governments into systematically selecting projects in ways that enhance well-being. Relatively resource-rich municipalities and private sector actors are popular project partners due to their reliability in being able to absorb earmarked funds and manage them well, but investing in them tends to benefit an already wealthy group of citizens rather than the poorest. At the same time, the Commission lacks both the capacity and the incentives to push more forcefully for member states to promote social goals. As I argue throughout Chapter Two and Chapter Three, these incentives increase the likelihood of 'Matthew effects', meaning that those who are already better off benefit the most from social investments. Matthew effects are known to have adverse effects on economic inequality, especially in corporatist-type welfare states (Cantillon, 2011).

To be clear, I am not arguing that GDP is insignificant in the study of EU spending. My position is that a better understanding of the effects of EU spending on intra-regional socio-economic inequalities between citizens is essential if well-informed decisions are to be made about the future.

The empirical context: EU regional policy

EU regional policy revolves around a range of what are nowadays known as the European Structural and Investment Funds. The oldest were the European Social Fund (ESF) and the European Agricultural Guidance and Guarantee Fund – Guidance Section (EAGGF-Guidance). The ESF dates back to the Treaty of Rome of 1958 and the EAGGF-Guidance was established in 1962. The European Regional Development Fund (ERDF) was created in 1975 and is commonly seen as the origin of the EU's current regional policy. In 1993, the Financial Instrument for Fisheries Guidance (FIFG) became the main pillar of the Common Fisheries Policy, and a Cohesion Fund was created aimed at the poorest member states. Member states may also avail themselves of a reformed and simplified European Agricultural Fund for Rural Development (EAFRD) and a European Maritime and Fisheries Fund (EMFF). All of these have, since 2007, been collectively referred to as the European Structural and Investment Funds. When I refer to EU regional policy, I mean the set of EU policies pursued through all the discussed funds.

Since a major reform in 1992, about a third of the EU budget has been set aside for EU regional funding, allocated with several objectives in mind, and with a set of conditions attached with which the Commission and the member states must comply (see Chapter Two). Historically, EU regional policy was intended to mitigate socio-economic divisions between EU regions caused by a range of national and global factors, most notably post-war deindustrialization, technological specialization and external economic shocks. Ever since the Treaty of Rome, EU regional policy has pursued a goal of reducing economic inequalities between regions. The Single European Act of 1986 introduced the objective of 'social and economic cohesion' and considerably increased the financial resources available, making regional funds the second-largest expenditure item behind the Common Agricultural Policy.

Thus, for a long time, cohesion has become associated by default with differences in regional performance (Begg, 2003), not between citizens within regions. Over time, however, the understanding of what cohesion entails has gradually changed and now increasingly includes inequalities between

for nationalist populism (Rodrik, 2018). The findings of this book suggest that reforming EU spending to buttress regional well-being should be part and parcel of work to counteract adverse spending effects on well-being in poor regions, and to strengthen citizens' beliefs in the legitimacy of the EU.

TWO

Social Goals in EU Regional Development Policy

EU regional policy appears to be a fertile ground for the integration of social goals such as poverty alleviation and social inclusion. It has a long history of pursuing social cohesion and an emphasis on active labour market policies, such as supporting vocational training schemes and micro-entrepreneurs, that resonates well with the idea of social investment. However, social investment is widely seen as a part of domestic welfare state policy, and there is strong pressure for this to remain in the hands of national governments (de la Porte and Natali, 2018).

Against this background, this chapter provides an in-depth analysis of the integration of social goals into EU regional policy, in terms of both formal rules and practice. A growing number of scholars have called for a more integrated approach by the EU that promotes growth and social goals at the same time (Vandenbroucke et al, 2011; Hemerijck, 2013; Heins and de la Porte, 2014; Aranguiz, 2019). Nonetheless, there has been no comprehensive analysis of the degree to which social goals have really been integrated into EU regional policy, which after all is the EU's main tool to enhance growth.

This chapter fills that gap. It provides an overview of how the regional fund implementation processes function and analyses social 'mainstreaming' in EU regional policy. The concept of mainstreaming is useful here as it refers to the integration of issues into the institutions and policies of a particular organization. The term has been used extensively in the literatures on gender (Hafner-Burton and Pollack, 2009) and EU environmental mainstreaming in the EU (Dupont,

2016), but not yet in the context of social and regional policies. I discuss how and when social goals have been mainstreamed into EU regional policy and the European Structural and Investment Funds that undergird that policy. By way of conclusion, the chapter discusses implications for the EU's ability to pursue social goals in its growth policies.

Regional policymaking

While 1988 is considered the watershed of EU regional policy, the 1992 reform taking effect in 1993 in conjunction with the Maastricht Treaty strengthened the goal of economic and social cohesion in regional policy as we know it today. The resources allocated to regional policy in the period 1988–93 were doubled to one fifth of the Community budget, making the structural funds the second-largest area of expenditure after the Common Agricultural Policy (Bache, 1998, ch. 4). Since 1993, EU funding has amounted to more than one third of the EU budget and has been ever since allocated in accordance with a number of objectives, each of which comes with a set of conditions with which the Commission and the member states must comply. There has been extensive discussion of the history of EU regional fund conditionality, governance and meanings of 'cohesion' (Rumford, 2000; Sutcliffe, 2000; Evans, 2005; Tödtling-Schönhofer et al, 2014; Bachtler et al, 2018, 2019; Bachtler and Begg, 2017; Mendez et al, 2019). I therefore only briefly outline the main aspects of relevance to my study.

The EU regulatory framework is divided into objectives funded through the various European Structural and Investment Funds: the ERDF, ESF, EAFRD, EMFF and the Cohesion Fund. These funds are used to pursue a number of objectives. Key to understanding these objectives is a major distinction made by the EU between 'Objective 1' or 'Convergence' regions, which have a GDP per capita of less than 75 per cent of the EU average, and the more prosperous regions that remain outside of Objective 1. Table 2.1 provides an overview of the development of the various funding objectives over time.

Between 1994 and 1999, the budget for EU regional policy amounted to roughly ECU 153 billion. Objective 1 was aimed at the regions that lagged behind in terms of GDP per capita. This objective covered about 70 per cent of the total regional policy budget. Objectives 2–4 were geared towards regions in industrial decline that were facing challenges pertaining to unemployment and unequal employment opportunities for young people, women and men. About 15 per cent of funding was allocated to these objectives. The remainder was allocated to Objective 5 and minor funding schemes, and mostly targeted at adaptation to changes in production systems and modernization of the agricultural and fisheries sectors (European Union, 2008).

In the period 2000–06, the funds were simplified into three funding objectives. While Objectives 1 and 2 remained largely the same, Objective 1 now included the French overseas departments, the Azores, Madeira and the Canary Islands, by virtue of their ultra-peripheral status, as well as areas of low population density in Austria, Finland and Sweden. Objective 2 funding continued to target regions in circumstances not covered by Objective 1 but now also emphasized deprived urban areas with structural difficulties linked, for example, to high levels of unemployment and social exclusion. Objective 3 funding was redesigned to promote adaptation and modernization policies and programmes related to education, vocational training and employment. Approximately €195 billion was set aside for the period 2000–06, with a similar division of resources between the objectives as in the preceding funding period (European Council, 1999).

The objectives were again reformed at the beginning of the 2007–13 budgetary period. Objective 1 was renamed 'Convergence' and Objective 2 became 'Regional Competitiveness and Employment' (RCE), but the eligibility criteria did not significantly change. A new Objective 3 was

Table 2.1: EU funding objectives and earmarked funding

Period	Description of funding objectives	Typical funding targets	Funds	Earmarked funds in current prices
1994–99	(1) Structural adjustment of lagging regions; (2) Regions in industrial decline; (3) Combat long-term unemployment; (4) Actions to prevent unemployment; (5a–b) Modernization of agricultural structures and rural areas; (6) Development of scarcely populated regions.	(1) Industrial and transport infrastructure; (2) Training of managers and firm owners; (3) Vocational education; (4) Retraining of workers; (5a) Manufacture of farm products; (5b) Processing of agricultural products; (6) Transportation infrastructure.	(1) ERDF, ESF, EAGGF-G (2) ERDF, ESF (3–4) ESF (5a) EAGGF-G, FIFG (5b-6) ERDF, ESF, EAGGF-G	(1) and (6) ECU 96 bn (2) ECU 7 bn (3–4) ECU 14 bn (5) ECU 12 bn *Total EU regional policy budget*: ECU 141 bn
2000–2006	(1) Structural adjustment of lagging regions; (2) Socio-economic reconversion of regions, not eligible under (1); (3) Support for the modernization of education, training and employment policies.	(1) Industrial and transport infrastructure; (2) Purchase of property to expand business premises; (3) Employee vocational training programme.	(1) ERDF, ESF, EAGGF-Guidance, FIFG (2) ERDF, ESF (3) ESF	(1): €136 bn (2): €23 bn (3): €24 bn *Total EU regional policy budget*: €195 bn
2007–13	(1) Convergence; (2) Regional competitiveness and employment.	(1) Industrial and transport infrastructure; (2) Vocational education and social inclusion.	(1) ERDF, ESF, Cohesion Fund (2) ERDF, ESF	(1): €252 bn (2): €49 bn *Total EU regional policy budget*: €308 bn

Period	Description of funding objectives	Typical funding targets	Funds	Earmarked funds in current prices
2014–20	11 thematic objectives: (1) Research and innovation; (2) Information and communication technologies; (3) SME competitiveness; (4) Low carbon economy; (5) Climate change adaption and risk management; (6) Environment and resource efficiency; (7) Sustainable transport and network bottlenecks; (8) Employment and labour mobility; (9) Social inclusion and poverty; (10) Education; (11) Institutional capacity.	(1) Promote centres of competence; (2) Support broadband deployment; (3) Coaching of SME owners; (4) Support renewable energy use in firms; (5) Support development of disaster risk management systems; (6) Waste sector projects; (7) Railway reparations; (8) Support micro-enterprises; (9) Investing in health infrastructure; (10) Vocational youth assistance; (11) More efficient social services.	All objectives: ERDF, ESF, Cohesion Fund	Investment for growth and jobs: €313 bn European Territorial Cooperation: €9 bn *Total*: €325 bn

Notes: Figures might not add up precisely to the total due to rounding, and as only funding schemes allocated to individual regions are shown; other excluded schemes represent less than 5 per cent of the total earmarked funds. EAGGF-G refers to EAGGF-Guidance. Small and medium enterprises (SMEs). Commission of the European Communities (1994); Council Regulation (EEC) No 2081/93; Council Regulation (EC) No 1260/1999 of 21 June 1999; Council Regulation (EC) No 1083/2006 of 11 July 2006, and Regulation (EU) No 1303/2013 of the European Parliament and of the Council of 17 December 2013.

created on 'European Territorial Cooperation', which targeted cross-border programmes and not individual regions. Along with the new programme names, budgetary resources were increased significantly. While €308 billion earmarked for the structural funds budget, once again the shares allocated to the different objectives remained largely unchanged. The share of resources available to the Convergence objective was increased to roughly 82 per cent while the resources available for the RCE objective decreased to approximately 16 per cent (articles 18–21 of Council regulation 1083/2006).

In the period 2014–20, roughly €325 billion was earmarked for regional policy. The main change was the creation of 11 thematic goals and the category of 'transition regions', for those regions with a per capita income of 75–90 per cent of the EU average. Despite these changes to the objectives, resources for the ESF, through which the bulk of social investments flows, still constituted less than 20 per cent of total funding.

Project funding

The funding objectives are pursued in a complex implementation process within the member states. The implementation process rests on three main legal principles. According to the 'principle of concentration', poor regions must receive more funding than rich regions. Importantly, poor regions also receive higher co-funding rates (around 80 per cent) from the EU than rich regions (around 50 per cent). For the newly introduced transition regions in 2014, the co-financing rate is 60 per cent. The 'partnership principle' means that regions must be included in the allocation process and that the Commission plays an advisory role, albeit with formal powers to approve investment plans. In line with the principle of 'additionality', EU funds must leverage and not displace or replace domestic funding from private and public sector sources. The idea is that EU funding should promote additional domestic spending beyond existing domestic spending programmes, and should not 'crowd out' or replace domestic spending (Evans, 2005).

The project funding process has three main stages (Tödtling-Schönhofer et al, 2014).[1] The *first stage* is related to 'programming'. Subnational and national authorities are required to draw up seven-year investment plans for each region, as well as a number of national plans with a regional dimension. These documents are referred to as Operational Programmes (OPs). OPs are formulated separately for different funds, such as the ERDF and the ESF. After 2007, these OPs had to fit within an overarching national investment strategy within a 'National Strategic Reference Framework'. This is a strategy document that draws together the funding objectives and priorities of all the regions. This document was replaced by a Partnership Agreement in 2014, which requires more detailed and coherent regional investment strategies related to the goals of Europe 2020, which are discussed further in the chapter. The investment plans must also comply with specific rules associated with the thematic concentration of funds and the rules on the three legal principles discussed. The Commission advises member states throughout this process and makes formal approval decisions on the final OPs.

The *second stage* involves assigning responsibilities for implementation. In EU regional policy parlance, the 'managing authorities' and 'payment authorities' are selected, respectively. In some EU member states, such as Germany and Spain, it is the regions that coordinate the OPs and funding and merely consult the federal government, which will also be managing several other OPs. In other states, such as Bulgaria and Romania, regions lack the institutional capacity to manage regional programmes, so regional projects are funded under the auspices of top-down national programmes.[2] In any case, project selection and the administrative processes of project management are often separate. For example, in France the *Préfet de Region* makes decisions on project funding but funding is included in the financial accounts of various regional policy areas. In Germany, the various regional ministries both make decisions on and manage the investments.[3] Intermediate bodies such as state-owned banks support project formulation and selection.

The *third and final stage* involves the implementation of co-financed projects by way of selection, monitoring, auditing and evaluation. Regional and national authorities select projects for EU funding based on the OPs and in consultation with the Commission. The final beneficiaries are typically businesses, civil society organizations, government authorities and research institutions at the local, regional and national levels. Authorities often identify promising projects in the region when they draw up the OPs, and include them strategically to increase the absorption rate of regional funding. An N+2 rule was applied between 2003 and 2013, according to which unspent funds should flow back into the EU budget within two years of the deadline for completing the project. Although this was replaced by an 'N+3' rule in 2014, this puts pressure on regional authorities to identify project partners early on in the programming period.[4]

The German-Turkish Economic Centre (*Deutsch-Türkisches Wirtschaftszentrum*) in Mannheim is a typical example of a social investment project. It is a non-governmental organization that supports local entrepreneurs of Turkish descent by providing the information and expertise needed to manage micro-businesses and to enhance equality of opportunity.[5] After consultation with the state-owned bank, *Landeskreditbank Baden-Württemberg*, which is responsible for assisting potential beneficiaries, the centre received €924,000 from the ERDF for infrastructure. This was leveraged by almost €700,000 from the City of Mannheim and €260,000 from the region of Baden-Württemberg, as well as €341,000 from the ESF for operating costs in 2002–06, leveraged by about €229,000 from the city, €273,000 from local welfare institutions, €21,000 from the local employment agency and €56,000 from the region's Chamber of Commerce (in current prices). Thanks to EU funding, the centre's services helped to build up 45 businesses, about 80 per cent of which were still operating after 1 year, and created more than 100 jobs (European Commission, 2010e). Partially due to its high operating costs, the project was not considered for EU funding in the period 2007–13.[6]

Social mainstreaming in EU regional policy

There are two main aspects of social mainstreaming in the context of regional policy. 'Regulatory mainstreaming' refers to the modification of formal and informal planning procedures, such as frameworks, regulations and policies at the start of a funding period. 'Implementation mainstreaming' has three aspects: (a) the integration of social issues into regional and multiregional plans as well as national investment plans with a regional dimension, OPs and projects, or 'programmatic mainstreaming'; (b) the modification of managerial and working structures, including internal formal and informal norms and job descriptions, and the configuration of sections or departments, or 'managerial mainstreaming'; and (c) a higher-level support to redirect the focus to social issues through use of European Commission soft power and technical assistance, or 'directed mainstreaming'.[7]

Regulatory mainstreaming

Since the Treaty of Rome, EU regional policies have pursued a goal of reducing economic inequalities between regions (Article 158 Treaty Establishing the European Community). The Single European Act of 1986 introduced the objective of 'social and economic cohesion' as a shared competence between EU member states and the EU institutions. The European Council confirmed its intention to create an Economic and Monetary Union (EMU) for the European Community at its June 1988 meeting. Just four months earlier, the European Community's heads of state and government had decided to cushion the progressive development of the EMU through the redistribution of fiscal resources at the European level.[8]

There was broad agreement among policymakers that fiscal redistribution from poor to rich states through the EU budget should endeavour to enhance social and economic cohesion. European leaders and their advisers drew up a new system of interconnected funds to promote growth, especially in regions that were lagging behind.[9] The predominant understanding of social cohesion in the EU regional policy community has historically been that increasing social and economic cohesion means reducing *inter*-regional inequalities. For example, the European Commission's *First Report on Economic and Social Cohesion* makes clear that cohesion means 'convergence of basic incomes through higher … [levels of] GDP growth, of competitiveness and of employment' (European Commission, 1996, p. 13).

In this book, I refer to 'social goals' as the reduction of *intra*-regional inequalities among people within regions. In the late 1980s and 1990s, there was already broad agreement among European policymakers that poor and otherwise vulnerable groups of citizens were likely to be hardest hit by market liberalization (European Commission, 1996, p. 116). It was widely believed that their well-being should be buttressed by deploying regional funds to strengthen the factors of production in their associated jurisdictions (European Commission, 1988; pp. 146–55, 174).[10] While there was not yet a majority in favour of allocating European funds directly to social investment projects, it was clear that the success of European redistribution would largely hinge on *both* 'their efficient use and … the private and social return on the investment programmes' (Delors, 1989, p. 19).

The impact of the 1990s economic recession led European policymakers to a realization that social investments through EU regional development funding needed to be better defined. Governments feared that European integration might boost economic growth but exacerbate social inequalities.

Throughout the 1990s, many elections in Europe were fought over conflicting views on welfare state reform – notably in Belgium, Germany and the Netherlands – but it was the Commission in particular that was intent on relating regional funding to issues of rising unemployment, social exclusion and urban deprivation. It was not until the late 1990s and early 2000s, however, that social investment thinking gained broader support among political entrepreneurs and governments (de la Porte and Natali, 2018).

Regional funding was reformed under the aegis of Agenda 2000. While Agenda 2000 is perhaps best known for tightening financial constraints, largely as a consequence of a refusal by the wealthier member states to finance the activities of the less well off, Agenda 2000 also mentioned promotion of the 'social model advocated by the European Union' in terms of public health, social inclusion, good employment conditions and the qualifications of young people (European Commission, 2000). This social model was anchored in the European Employment Strategy of 1997 and tied to regional policy. Regional funding was supposed to make 'a direct contribution to this by promoting restructuring and development and creating durable jobs ... attempting to equip young people, women and those who have been out of work for long spells to compete more effectively for employment' (European Commission, 1996, p. 116). More concretely, at the March 2000 European Council in Lisbon, the ESF was firmly integrated into the Lisbon Strategy. This strategy was essentially a 10-year plan for growth and jobs in the EU that also aimed to lift 20 million people out of poverty by 2020 (European Commission, 2014b).

The Lisbon Strategy made social investment an integral part of the regional funds, especially the ESF,[11] which had long been used to facilitate the geographical and occupational mobility of workers (Gordon, 1991). After 2000, ESF goals such as social inclusion, gender equality, tackling discrimination and lifelong learning became more pronounced and measurable through new indicators for poverty and social exclusion known as the 'Laeken indicators' (Barca, 2009).

The crisis years of 2007–12 saw a general trend for welfare state retrenchment in the developed world and a reorientation of public investment to traditional growth-enhancing policies. The 'Europe 2020' strategy of 2010, the successor to the Lisbon Strategy, placed Europe's pursuit of social inclusion, and reducing economic inequality and poverty among citizens as part of Europe's growth strategy, centre stage (European Commission, 2010a, 2010b, 2014a). Debates around EU growth now paid increased attention to *who benefits* from economic growth.[12] New initiatives for inclusive growth were adopted as part of Europe 2020, such as the Social Investment Package and the Youth Guarantee. However, these continued to rely on the 'open method of coordination' (OMC) (Heins and de la Porte, 2014).

The OMC is a term coined at the March 2000 Lisbon European Council to group together various types of EU soft law such as reporting, guidelines, indicators, 'naming and shaming' and sharing of best practices (Barcevicius et al, 2014). Thus, social goals pursued through the OMC did not become linked more closely to regional policy. What is more, during the crisis and its aftermath, regional policy was predominantly discussed not in relation to social investment but as a tool for economic crisis management.[13] It may thus come as no surprise that EU social investments have declined in Europe's poorer regions in the crisis years 2007–12.[14]

Taken together, these insights are evidence of the regulatory mainstreaming of social goals into EU regional policy since 1992, especially by extending and reformulating the social goals of the ESF in relation to the aims of the Lisbon Strategy in the period 2000–06 and tying them to intra-regional disparities in addition to inter-regional disparities. However, as established in the Introduction (Chapter One), social funding remains at about one fifth of the total regional policy budget. Efforts by the Commission linked to the 2000–06 framework to split regional funding evenly between social and economic goals did not gain member state support.[15] And, implementation mainstreaming remains fragmented and weak.

Implementation mainstreaming

Programmatic mainstreaming of social goals has been gradually strengthened since 2007. One signal change in the implementation process is that since the 2007–13 period, member states have been nudged into improving the coherence of their regional and investment strategies in respect of the various funds. At that time, the National Strategic Reference Framework required regional and national governments to outline how social and economic investment strategies could combine to meet regional challenges. In the 2014–20 period, member states had to devise a more detailed strategy on combining social and economic investments in a Partnership Agreement.

There is also evidence of directed mainstreaming, especially during the period 2000–06. When the Delors Commission was in office in the late 1980s and early 1990s, it was widely believed that regional policies would spur growth but also serve as a catalyst for deeper social and institutional change (Rumford, 2000, p. 163). It was not until the inception of the Lisbon Strategy that the Commission sought to engage in directed mainstreaming, providing coordination and technical assistance with distributing the funds and exerting soft power in the form of guidelines and discussion papers.[16] However, the Commission generally has only limited capacity or power to influence project selection (Pollack, 2003), which is a politically sensitive topic.[17] It is the regional and national public authorities that ultimately control the selection of projects (Bache, 1998) and the Commission depicts project selection as a domestic and technical matter.[18] In fact, the Commission tends only to have knowledge of the larger, successful projects.[19]

To illustrate, the Commission receives all OPs for approval more or less at the same time – 400 or 500 depending on the period – and about a handful of mid-level Commission officials then assess them and negotiate them one at a time with the member state concerned. As the Commission is involved in preparing the closure of the previous period at the same time, it is typically hard-pressed to get everything done, leaving little room for checking the content of investment plans. Commission influence on investment plans is instead achieved through the provision of funding guidelines at the outset of a funding period; but these are typically disseminated quite late on when OPs are already being formulated and capacity limitations mean that project partners are already being identified.[20] Additional political pressure can occur where domestic actors deliberately delay the revision of OPs to push the Commission into accepting them. This happened for instance in the context of a major inter-regional (Interreg) programme between Portugal and Spain, which accounted for about 20 per cent of all the European resources allocated to Interreg in the period 2000–06.[21]

Another strategy for creating fertile ground for directed mainstreaming is to increase the flexibility of the OPs to facilitate using EU funds in ways that build on the broad objectives of the Lisbon Strategy.[22] This has been a goal since 2007 in particular, but such flexibility can have adverse effects. It allows the regions to continue to use EU funds largely as they see fit. While projects should be broadly in line with the OPs, the Commission has neither the means nor the power to sanction projects that are not. As a result, many – perhaps even most – projects co-funded by and declared to the Commission are not part of a deliberate strategy to promote EU social investment goals.[23]

Finally, managerial mainstreaming is largely absent. EU regional policy has certainly brought about decentralization in Europe (Hooghe et al, 2016), promoting an ideal of an 'autonomous region' (Rumford, 2000), but regional and social policy departments are typically siloed even in the newly created regional authorities, which constitutes an important barrier to social mainstreaming.

Conclusion

There has been a vivid debate in recent years about the limits of traditional growth policies and their effects on political polarization in the EU (Collier, 2018; Stiglitz et al, 2018). Nonetheless, social and regional policies remain almost entirely separate. Social norms and values are mainly being diffused through the OMC (Ferrera, 2017), and economic thinking that advocates keeping social and growth policies separate remains widespread (Farole et al, 2011).

The mainstreaming of social goals into regional policy through regulation and implementation may have become increasingly common since the early 1990s, but the EU's social investment portfolio has remained largely unchanged. Capacity issues, the small amounts of EU social funding involved and member states' power to use social investments largely as they see fit once the money has been earmarked present major challenges to the coherence of an EU social investment policy that seeks to benefit the poorest.

I argue in the following Chapter Three that this weak mainstreaming of social goals into EU regional policy will restrict the effects of its social investment and encourage regions to channel social investments to their already skilled and relatively wealthy societal groups, which could even have adverse effects on income inequality. This argument is evidenced in Chapter Five and Chapter Six, where I demonstrate some salutary effects of EU social funding on well-being in the more prosperous regions, alongside adverse effects on income inequality in poorer regions.

THREE

A Theory of EU Spending and Regional Well-Being

The time could not be more propitious to examine how EU spending can be used to promote well-being. More and more people in Europe are debating what the EU can do for the citizens of its member states, and what benefits it has really generated on their behalf. We live in an era of increasing public debate about the EU (Hooghe and Marks, 2009), where populist rhetoric is regularly deployed to exacerbate people's anxieties and threat perceptions linked to economic insecurity (Hameleers et al, 2017). The UK's decision to leave (so-called Brexit) has shown how economic divides have contributed to an erosion of favourable attitudes towards the EU, underlining that citizens care deeply about distributional issues (Algan et al, 2017).

Little is known about the extent to which EU spending actually improves people's lives, despite notable evaluation studies (Bachtler et al, 2013, 2019). Most research on EU regional funding effects focuses on gross domestic product (GDP) growth or convergence. This approach is attractive insofar as it expresses a society's wealth in a single measure. However, it neither considers the distribution of wealth nor the well-being and future prospects of individual people. The central argument in this chapter is about the effects of EU social investment in individuals at different stages of the life course on regional well-being. I argue that where EU spending reaches poor and otherwise disadvantaged people, by strengthening capabilities, it will enhance regional well-being. Under the current legal framework, however, and in the light of existing funding practices, more prosperous areas within the regions and the wealthier segments of society receive most of the benefits.

The chapter begins by proposing a concept of 'regional well-being' in the sense of a state of distributive justice in the regions, in which every individual has the capability to achieve the quality of life they are striving for. It then develops the argument by drawing on insights in political philosophy and welfare economics. The chapter closes by discussing the context factors that govern how EU spending effects unfold.

Conceptualizing regional well-being

To define regional well-being, it is useful to consider previous conceptions of well-being offered in well-being research. *Subjective* notions of well-being – often referred to as 'a good quality of life', a person's 'welfare', or 'a person's good' – are concerned with individual cognitive and/or affective states. Alternatively, conceptions of well-being as *social* relations rest on the belief that a focus on individual interiority is inappropriate for capturing the individual intersubjective circumstances that enhance well-being. *Objective* well-being, by contrast, refers to the contextual factors that are assumed to enhance well-being.

Most studies of subjective well-being have notions of happiness and life satisfaction at their core. From this perspective, well-being has a cognitive component, life satisfaction, and an affective component, happiness (Eger and Maridal, 2015). Subjective well-being theory rests on three main assumptions (Carruthers and Hood, 2004). First, that well-being as a reflection of quality of life, or how good a life feels to the person who is living it, is dependent on just one factor – that person's happiness. The happier they are, the better their life; and the unhappier they are, the worse. Second, that happiness is the ultimate aim for which humans should strive. Other values, such as human development, social capital or public health, are just seen as contributing to this overarching value (Jordan, 2008). Third, that a person's well-being consists solely of having the right kind of mental state, which means that it is possible to assess individual well-being entirely 'from the inside' without reference to surrounding social conditions (Sumner, 1996, p. 157).

While some argue that the subjective ought to be the ultimate 'dependent variable' in the social sciences (Helliwell and Putnam, 2007, p. 435), the assumption that the roots of happiness are immaterial has been the subject of particular scrutiny. Such an assumption can propagate paradoxical situations, particularly when a delusional person's feelings of happiness arise from a radical misperception of their life circumstances. It would be counterintuitive, if not illogical, to conclude in such circumstances that a person is living a good-quality life. Whether human beings are capable of truly knowing their own condition is certainly an open question, as debates about thought experiments such as the 'brain in a vat' test demonstrate (Putnam, 1981, pp. 1–21).

Other critical voices contend that collective well-being only ever partially shapes personal well-being, and for this reason measures of individual happiness elide crucial aspects of well-being (Keyes and Lopez, 2002). This basic insight is consistent with the 'Easterlin Paradox', which rests on Richard Easterlin's (1995) finding that average national happiness does not appear to increase in the long term even in the face of substantial increases in per capita income.

Based on insights from this well-being research, I propose a concept of *regional well-being*. My goal is to introduce an understanding of distributive equity as 'distributive justice' into the debate on EU spending. Distributive equity within regions deals with what individuals in particular circumstances are entitled to as a share of society's production. Equity is therefore not the same as equality. Equality is typically understood as treating individuals in the same way in some form of distribution of resources. By contrast, equity requires that individual well-being be defined by the justice inherent in an income distribution.

Turning to political philosophy for assistance, the theory most often invoked in discussions of equity is John Rawls' (1971) conception of 'distributive justice as fairness', a liberal theory of justice that has been diffused throughout the academic world and beyond. At the risk of oversimplifying, Rawls' theory of distributive justice is based on two principles, the second of which has two main parts. The first principle states that each person should be able to enjoy an equal level of basic liberties. The second holds that socio-economic inequalities are justified only if they are: (a) tied to offices and positions that are open to anyone under conditions of equal opportunity [fair equality of opportunity]; and (b) most beneficial to the least advantaged members of society [difference principle]. In other words, (a) inequalities are acceptable to the extent that the higher incomes accorded to the talented and the hard-working are achieved under a condition of equal opportunities, regardless of whether people are born rich or poor. What is more, (b) views economic inequalities as justified, but only insofar as these inequalities can lead to increases in the incomes of the lowest earners (Rawls, 1993, pp. 5–6, 2001, p. 43; see, for a more in-depth discussion of the implications of these principles for social policy, Rothstein, 1998).

This line of thinking – which is often referred to as the 'maximin principle' – embodies the precept that a society's wealth is only as great as the welfare of the worst-off individual. It is also based on the belief that differences in individual talents, income and wealth can be used in a way that makes everyone, and especially the poorest, better off. In short, a just distribution is achieved by maximizing the welfare of the worst-off.

Building on this conception of distributive justice, I suggest that regional development and inequalities in the EU should be discussed as distributive justice in terms of an obligation of EU funding and associated domestic spending to make the poorest citizens better off. The more a given income distribution benefits the worst-off, the more just the distribution.

In addition, I argue that distributive justice should not only be understood as the availability of resources for individuals. By contrast, we should focus on the factors enabling individual *capabilities* to use these resources to accomplish the life they value (Sen, 1985). The general problem with approaches to EU spending prioritizing resource availability is that such approaches overestimate the importance of resources and distract from what is really important, that is, the relationship between resources and people. Following Sen (1989), this is the case even if these resources might be broadly conceived as 'primary goods' that individuals normally prefer more, rather than less of, such as natural (like intelligence and health) and social (like civic freedom and income) goods (Rawls, 1971).

It is important to note that the conception of regional well-being differs from what is termed 'equality of opportunity'. According to the theory of fair allocations, it is necessary to distinguish between 'unfair' inequalities, which are brought about by factors such as social class or origin over which individuals have no control, and 'fair' inequalities, which are ethically defensible insofar as they result from factors over which individuals can exert control, such as the effects of alcohol consumption on health (Rothstein, 1998, pp. 50–53). It is obviously the case that the concept of control may not be static, as individuals may be able to exert more or less control during the course of their lifetimes. In addition, problems with habits that negatively affect health are more often found among vulnerable social groups (Marmot, 2004).

Much of the pertinent literature distinguishes between relative and absolute approaches to poverty (Sen, 1985; Son, 2011). A related relative concept is 'pro-poor growth', which is commonly defined as a situation in which poverty declines more than it would have if all incomes increased at the same rate (Kakwani et al, 2004). According to the absolute approach, growth is presumptively pro-poor if the living standards of those classified as poor have improved (Foster, 1998).

Based on these insights, I assume that a just distribution of income within regions is achieved by improving the lot of the worst-off relative to other citizens. A more just distribution of income will thus make it more likely that individuals with the same degree of talent and ambition – but with a different economic status – have the same prospects of achieving their goals. It is the distribution of income together with individual capabilities that matters for well-being.

So which capabilities do citizens need to achieve a good quality of life that they value? There is no predetermined, much less a canonical, list of capabilities that theorists can use devoid of input from wider society. Different capabilities must instead be exposed to context-specific inquiry. The basic ingredients of individual well-being are interrelated social and economic factors that are conducive to individual capabilities to achieve well-being. Such capabilities are not just about basic economic needs; they are also about the lives people are able to lead (Son 2011, p. 13). I understand bad health, unemployment and other forms of disadvantage as deprivations of the capabilities essential to the successful pursuit of the good things in life (Raveaud and Salais, 2001).

Globalization, technology and regional well-being

Before developing my theoretical framework on the effects of EU social investments on regional well-being, it is useful to establish the global and supranational contexts in which my argument about EU spending effects on well-being unfolds. Globalization and European integration are trends that have ubiquitously contributed to a transformation of contemporary European societies (Beckfield, 2019).

A common narrative has it that changes in income inequality can be attributed to growing trade interdependence among states across the globe. From this perspective, demand has shifted from unskilled to skilled labour as a result of the liberalization of capital and of the supply of goods. This shift has had deleterious distributional consequences, including on income equality (Kremer, 2006). These distributional consequences have been inflicted by technology diffusion and the resulting shifts in demand in the labour market that globalization brings about. An increased prevalence of advanced technology increases the demand for highly skilled employees. At the same time, technology diffusion can also increase unemployment among the lower skilled, thereby adversely affecting distributive justice.

This logic is bolstered by two well-known economic theories, the Heckscher-Ohlin and the Stolper-Samuelson, which state that expanded opportunities for trade heighten the comparative advantage of those industrial sectors with skill-intensive outputs. At the subnational level, the effects of shifts in the demand for skilled labour are likely to be more pronounced in regions that have undergone the greatest technological change. Regions with greater levels of technology uptake are more likely to have a higher demand for high-skilled than low-skilled labour, which can increase economic inequality and thus undermine regional well-being. However, the impact of development on regional income distribution could be non-linear, in that positive effects on equality may be discernible at low levels of development and adverse effects at high levels of development (Castells-Quintana et al, 2015).

Kuznets' hypothesis on the effect of industrialization on income inequality is helpful on this point. Simon Kuznets (1955) famously articulated the argument that industrialization and urbanization lead to both economic development and economic inequality. The inverted 'Kuznets curve' predicts that a small cohort of wealthy individuals will emerge in urban industrialized areas in less developed countries. Urbanization and industrialization are expected to lead both to growth and to declines in income inequality within regions resulting from an increased demand for high-skilled and specialized labour.

The empirical support for this hypothesis in inequality research is, however, mixed at best.

In terms of individual capacities to achieve well-being, greater trade liberalization can have a positive impact on overall public health, since socio-economic development can lead to improvements in both infrastructure and the provision of goods and services (Lange and Vollmer, 2017). Indeed, Chapter Five will show that socio-economic development in the EU is indeed associated with lower infant mortality rates, indicating better healthcare and the consumption of nutritious food.

Moreover, the relationship between regional growth and inequality could be spurious when public policies are taken into account (Pontusson, 2005). Such policies can be global or European. Jason Beckfield (2019) has argued convincingly that it is important to distinguish between global and European integration trends. The EU's public debt rules, which are widely associated with 'austerity' politics, have been a powerful constraint on public spending. European integration promotes economic stability and growth, rather than income equality.

The debate on the impacts of political-economic processes related to globalization and European integration on domestic welfare states continues. The following sections build on insights from this literature to develop my argument about the causal mechanisms through which I expect EU social investment to shape regional well-being, and how the effect varies according to the economic, political and social circumstances in regions.

EU social investment and regional well-being

My theory on the relationship between EU social investments and regional well-being builds on previous research on distributive justice, welfare states and welfare economics. These three bodies of work offer rich and complementary insights that are seldom drawn together. By linking these research traditions, I seek to give the concept of well-being analytical depth and to make a stronger case for the EU attending to both capabilities and distributive justice within its borders. Both of these aspects of well-being are inextricably linked, and we need to understand how the EU should target its investments in a context-sensitive manner in order to promote them.

There is a basic premise that EU social investments can only make a difference to those aspects of people's lives for which those with political power, rather than the people themselves, are responsible. Individual citizens are responsible for their own aspirations, decision making and actions, and should have the capability to control these facets of their lives (Sen, 1985). Nonetheless, societies are unlikely to increase well-being unless citizens' elected representatives and other politically powerful actors contribute to its attainment (Rawls 1993, p. 268).[1] In the absence of governments taking responsibility, market failures would lead to suboptimal intra-regional distributions of income, in terms of the quantity of services produced and consumed, and as manifest, for example, in healthcare, educational and monetary benefits. Governments at all levels of the European multilevel polity have a shared responsibility to promote regional well-being. My model of well-being differences concerns those factors which are beyond the realm of personal control, and therefore responsibility.

Capabilities

EU social investments seek to promote regional well-being by strengthening the individual capabilities of poor and otherwise disadvantaged people. The basic idea behind social investments is that they aim to promote the development of individual capabilities throughout life (Busemeyer et al, 2018). This idea has influenced EU spending policies particularly between 1997, the year of the adoption of the European Employment Strategy, and 2013, as Lazlo Andor, Commissioner for Employment, Social Affairs and Inclusion in the second Barroso Commission from 2010–14, one of the key political entrepreneurs advocating for social investments, left the Commission the year after (de la Porte and Natali, 2018). By contrast, economic investments primarily seek to improve competitiveness or, in other words, promote efficiency through capital subsidies.

The causal mechanism linking EU social investments and regional well-being lies at the individual level. Supply-side investment in the development of capabilities, especially skills, among those who are poor or otherwise disadvantaged helps to enhance a region's stock of human capital from among the poor. At the same time, employment policies have been shown to influence workforce participation rates of groups at the margins of the labour market, notably the long-term unemployed (Bassanini and Duval, 2006). Young people who do not go to school might receive vocational training that makes them more employable. The long-term unemployed might be given the opportunity to participate in labour market programmes intended to ease their return to the workforce. Greater investment in educational inputs, especially benefiting households containing children and young people, where key decisions on human capital investment are most often made, will improve educational attainment and enhance the skills of young people and the workforce overall (OECD, 2014). In this way, investing in capabilities might also make it more likely that gains in social inclusion and health will be achieved.

In addition, EU social investment could help to reduce inequality if it were used to effectively assist innovative entrepreneurs and public bodies to promote public educational and employment opportunities of benefit to poor and otherwise disadvantaged societal groups. If the public benefits of educational investments outweigh the personal benefits for the affected individuals – as manifest, for instance, in individual wage increases – then socio-economic inequalities can be reduced (Boix, 1998). Better-distributed educational opportunities have a positive effect on income equality, which means that governments can play a meaningful role in this area through the deployment of social protection transfers (Salverda et al, 2011; Busemeyer, 2014).

Institutions and funding practices

Current rules mostly benefit wealthy urbanized areas, and within these their highly skilled populations benefit the most (Mohl and Hagen, 2011). That it is often the already wealthy actors that are able to capitalize on social investments is a prominent criticism in welfare state research (Cantillon, 2011). Similarly, EU social investments are at present unlikely to be powerful instruments for combating poverty and income inequality, as they target an already wealthy and skilled societal segment in a phenomenon known as the 'Matthew effect'. Given such Matthew effects, social investments might even contribute to increasing inequalities (Busemeyer et al, 2018).[2]

The existing institutions and practices in which EU fund management is embedded provide powerful incentives for regional and national governments to invest primarily in already wealthy areas and their relatively rich inhabitants. Competency in EU funds management was increasingly granted to public bodies and stakeholders at the subnational level as EU regional policy underwent a series of reforms, especially after 1993, which brought about profound institutional changes that empowered regional authorities (Hooghe, 1996; Bache, 1998). Power-sharing between public bodies at the regional, national and supranational levels has become an increasingly institutionalized practice in the EU, with the exception of unitary and centralized states such as Denmark, Luxembourg and Malta which do not have a strong subnational tier of government (Hooghe et al, 2016). Regional and national government autonomy – often called 'subsidiarity' – in EU funds management is now standard practice.

It is the mark of a practice that actors widely accept institutional rules as defining the practice, making it a stable reference point for action (Rawls, 1955, p. 24). Government autonomy is thus embedded in the EU institutions through a persistent and connected set of European and domestic rules that prescribe behavioural roles, constrain activity and shape expectations. In practice, autonomy means that regional and national governments have much leeway to decide which projects are funded through the EU budget. Domestic governments certainly have the advantage of better access to local information about conditions, which means that their decisions on the provision of local public goods are likely to reflect local needs better than decisions made by the Commission.

Nonetheless, subsidiarity presents several challenges. To begin with, the autonomy of domestic governments opens up space for the retention of variations in pre-existing spending practices among EU member states, which can undermine EU social goals. As a result, social goals are often mentioned but not firmly anchored in EU funding practices (de la Porte and Natali, 2018). Moreover, the authorities managing EU funds have an unequivocal incentive to use up earmarked funds, which would otherwise flow back into the EU budget. Since the 2000–06 multiannual funding period, so-called decommitment rules have been put in place to ensure that funds 'committed' or earmarked in the EU budget that are not spent on projects at the end of two (since 2014, three) years following the year of allocation – the 'N+2' or 'N+3' rule – are lost. This has enabled strategies to fund strong projects by powerful actors that are anticipated to be able to absorb the funds applied for (OECD, 2020b).

High absorption rates are also attractive for the Commission, which is politically responsible for ensuring implementation of the EU budget. It faces powerful political incentives to avoid the risk of financial means flowing back to the EU budget. By implication, the Commission supports funding that benefits areas or actors with a demonstrably high capacity to adequately plan and absorb EU funds, as it is formally responsible for the correct implementation of the EU budget (Dellmuth, 2011a).

This strategy is perfectly in line with growth-enhancing investment but at odds with explicit spending goals such as poverty alleviation and social inclusion.

Given that under the current legal framework EU social investments tend to benefit rich areas, powerful project partners and highly skilled populations, EU social investments can have positive net employment effects in regions with favourable conditions for funding but still exacerbate income inequality. Intra-regional income inequality already tends to be higher in the metropolitan regions than in rural regions, given the relatively strong human capital stocks and the high demand for skilled labour (Boulant et al, 2016). EU social investments might thus be fuelling existing trends towards higher inequality within these regions.

Economic, political and social context conditions

Another angle on the politics of EU social investments and their effects on well-being focuses on the role of contextual conditions that support or obstruct EU spending effects. A framework for the posited relationships between EU social investments and well-being outcomes is embedded in the specific economic, political and social context. This shapes the ability of governments to put EU funds to good use, which previous literature has varyingly described as 'absorptive capacity', human capital or institutional capacity in a region (Begg, 2003; Becker et al, 2013).

Human capital refers to the skills of regional populations that are put to productive use (Becker et al, 2013). Such skills might consist of educational attainment, entrepreneurial activity, industry-specific employment and leadership experience at the individual level. Institutional quality could in a narrow sense pertain to political organizations such as public authorities or entities within authorities. In a broader sense, it is usefully described as the degree of social capital inherent in social institutions. Social capital is a feature of the structures that promote social trust, norms of reciprocity and, therefore, better-functioning networks that span the social, political and economic spheres (Putnam, 1993). Such networks are crucially important in the implementation of EU funding programs, as discussed later.

Human and social capital endowment are expected to enhance the effects of EU funding on regional well-being, each through a specific mechanism. The first mechanism is the existing human capital stock. Key here is the notion that investing in human capital through education and training can help to increase productivity and thus GDP growth and wages (Rodríguez-Pose and Fratesi, 2004). However, business owners may have a greater incentive to seek EU funding when their human capital stock is already relatively high, as returns on investment are higher in such circumstances. This insight suggests that EU funds may be more likely to have an impact on well-being in regions with a greater human capital endowment (cf Ederveen et al, 2006; Becker et al, 2013) and that are better situated to absorb EU funds in ways that improve outcomes relevant to regional well-being, such as better education, higher income and greater social inclusion. Moreover, a region that already possesses a stock of human capital can signal its capacity to enhance that endowment.

The second mechanism is social capital. Social capital might expand regional capacity in a manner that promotes greater and more efficient intra-regional networking among public and private sector actors – an instrumental factor in nurturing innovative and inclusive projects (cf Conzelmann, 1995; Tosun, 2013). Social capital promotes networks that are more likely to include representatives of disadvantaged communities or groups. Related research has shown that states, regions and cities with a more trusting populace tend to exhibit greater economic equality (Rothstein and Uslaner, 2005). In the context of EU funding, social capital might connect public and private actors that seek to improve the access of marginalized or low-skilled people to training opportunities, and to connect them in turn with organizations knowledgeable about how to design and implement effective projects for EU funding. Investing in such groups will enhance the positive effects of EU funds on regional well-being. These insights support the expectation that social capital, by improving inclusiveness, can reinforce EU funding effects on regional well-being.

Figure 3.1 illustrates that human and social capital endowments are significantly lower in relatively poor Objective 1 or Convergence regions than in relatively rich regions.[3] This corroborates the claim that regions experiencing substantial

Figure 3.1: Absorptive capacity in rich vs poor regions, 1993–2013

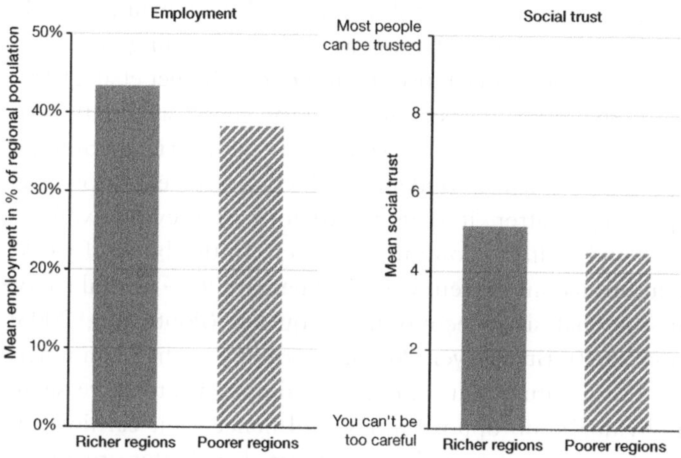

Notes: Human capital is measured as the economically active population per capita. Employment per capita is calculated as the proportion of employed persons aged 15 to 74 in the total regional population. Social capital refers to regional average social trust calculated by using post-stratification weights on the basis of European Social Survey (ESS) data (see www.europeansocialsurvey.org). Where missing due to biennial measurement in the ESS, it is replaced by mean trust between the measurements. Question posed: Using this card, generally speaking, would you say that most people can be trusted, or that you can't be too careful in dealing with people? Please tell me on a score of 0 to 10, where 0 means you can't be too careful and 10 means that most people can be trusted.

corruption and clientelism tend to lack the structure required to engender positive EU funding effects (Cappelen et al, 2003; Becker et al, 2013). It is interesting to note that trust in the EU is on average higher in poorer regions, where about 54 per cent of respondents trust the EU compared to about 48 per cent in richer regions. The proportion of people who trust the EU rose to more than 60 per cent during the global economic upswing of 2000–06 but fell to 48 per cent during the crisis years of 2007–12, while trust in the EU in richer regions remained at largely similar levels as in the 1990s.

When discussing political factors, national social and economic investments are naturally important (Begg, 2003). Social policy is the traditional preserve of the nation state, and patterns of domestic social investment have remained largely unchanged despite attempts at capacity building and ideas diffusion in EU social investment policy (Bouget et al, 2015).

EU spending effects on regional well-being are contingent on whether they are backed up by appropriate domestic social investments. To identify which categories of domestic spending matter, it is useful to look at previous welfare state and welfare economics research. In this body of work, educational investment is a – and perhaps *the* – central factor in the analysis of economic inequality (Pontusson, 2005; Son, 2010; Busemeyer, 2014). According to the main tenets of this literature, educational spending tends to increase an individual's job opportunities, and hence their earnings, as workers who are more highly educated are better situated to demand a higher wage than their less-educated counterparts. By improving people's skills, educational spending will increase educational attainment in preparation for a university or equivalent degree, which should be reflected in the wages of the better educated and in the distribution of income throughout society.

In addition, EU healthcare investment is likely to have an effect on citizens' physical security, both actual and self-perceived. Healthcare provision, such as the availability of doctors or hospital beds per capita, varies widely across EU regions (Eurostat, 2020), a fact recently highlighted during the rapid spread of the COVID-19 pandemic. To take one tangible exemplar, there are significantly fewer hospital beds per 1,000 inhabitants in relatively poor Objective 1 or Convergence regions than in richer regions.[4] I assume that EU healthcare investment can affect a region's health outcomes. These assumptions are reasonable given that existing studies have failed to show that EU spending has large 'crowding out' effects on national funding, as governments do not appear to systematically use EU funds to replace existing domestic spending (Alegre, 2012; Janský et al, 2016). This means that EU policies, leveraged by national spending, can have an effect on well-being.

Another factor at the national level that can have an important influence on EU funding effects is electoral politics. Previous research has convincingly shown that politicians interested in being re-elected are motivated to distribute EU funds to regions where there are relatively more core voters (Dellmuth et al, 2017). More generally, opportunistic governments are known to artificially stimulate the economy before general elections and take countervailing action afterwards. Since voters typically do not have a firm grasp of how the economy works, governments anticipate that they will be rewarded for this behaviour as the economy will be perceived to be performing well at the time of the election (e.g., Franzese, 2002).

In the context of EU spending, however, it is unlikely that electoral politics have undermining effects on well-being. Electoral politics may only undercut a potentially positive effect of EU funding on well-being, insofar as a government's immediate motivation does not conform with a funding rationale that positively influences well-being. However, previous studies have found either that only a small fraction of EU funding is ordinarily diverted to targeting voters in pursuit of electoral advantage (Kemmerling and Bodenstein, 2006; Dellmuth et al, 2017), or that there were no robust effects of electoral politics on the allocation of EU funds (Chalmers, 2013). EU regional fund allocations are rather reflective of the distributive conflicts between national governments and regions, and between recipient regions, than they are of party politics.

Conclusion

At the outset of the EU's long-term budget for 2021–27, it is important to scrutinize how EU institutions and domestic funding practices need to change in order to have more forceful and sustainable effects on well-being. At present, powerful incentives lead domestic authorities to spend EU funds mostly in wealthy areas. How to build incentive structures to promote inclusive growth continues to be one of the greatest challenges facing EU regional and social policy.

This chapter has developed a theoretical argument about the conditions under which EU regional spending will enhance regional well-being. Combining previous literature on distributive justice and welfare economics, the central argument is that EU spending benefiting poor and otherwise disadvantaged people, by strengthening their capabilities, will enhance regional well-being. The chapter has discussed the economic, social and political conditions under which such EU spending effects are likely to occur.

The following chapters will empirically examine this argument. Chapter Four will map well-being across regions and over time, placing particular emphasis on well-being trajectories during the 2007–12 crisis years. The results suggest that ostensibly successful regional economies in terms of economic growth continue to face formidable challenges related to intra-regional well-being. Chapter Five uses the quantitative dataset to explore the theoretical framework by way of regression analysis. Chapter Six further examines the regression results qualitatively, highlighting five central barriers to EU funding effects on well-being.

FOUR

Patterns of Regional Well-Being

Almost ten years after the 2007–12 global financial crisis, EU citizens are still feeling the effects of social and economic insecurities to the detriment of perceived distributive justice (Eurofound, 2018).* This underlines the need for an analysis of patterns of well-being that takes into account whether people live in poor or rich regions in the EU. In this chapter, I will analyse well-being by comparing poor and rich regions, drawing on the distinction in EU regional policy between relatively poor Objective 1 or Convergence regions, which have a GDP below 75 per cent of the EU average, and the richer regions outside of Objective 1 or Convergence.

Progress in the study of subnational well-being in the EU has to date been hampered by the absence of comprehensive datasets. This chapter therefore introduces a novel quantitative dataset that includes various measures of regional well-being as conceptualized in Chapter Three. I discuss how the well-being indicators were created and which data sources were used to compile the dataset, which is unique in its regional coverage over the period from 1994 to 2013. The dataset has been collated at the NUTS 1 and 2 levels, since it is at these levels that regional fund payments are appropriated and administered (see Table A.1). This allows me to examine the

* My thanks to Ognjen Zugic for his valuable contributions to this chapter.

various well-being problems encountered in regions that EU funding is intended to ameliorate.

After presenting the dataset, the chapter provides an analysis of patterns of well-being. This descriptive analysis reveals strong variations over time at the regional level both within and between EU member states, which underlines the importance of using regions as a unit of analysis in order to gain a nuanced understanding of well-being. There are two key findings. First, richer regions tend to perform better on all well-being indicators. Second, levels of poverty and income inequality have not significantly declined since the 1990s in either rich or poor regions. In the discussion of the results, the chapter pays specific attention to well-being trajectories in the crisis years of 2007–12.

Taking stock: existing measures of well-being

There is much debate surrounding the proper measurement of well-being. In welfare economics, many argue that gross domestic product (GDP) is a good proxy for well-being. Recent research has shown that regional eligibility for Convergence funding would not substantially change if the OECD's Well-Being Index rather than GDP were used as a primary indicator of regional socio-economic need (Döpke et al, 2017). These studies yield important insights but only insufficiently acknowledge that objective well-being is a complex and multidimensional concept.

Recent accounts have offered a number of broader approaches to operationalizing well-being as a multidimensional concept (see McGillivray and Shorroks, 2005; Barrington-Leigh and Escande, 2018). Measurement occurs either at the individual or the state level. Objective well-being measures typically capture economic, social and environmental circumstances. Health and educational status are the metrics most widely used in inter-state assessments of national attainment of well-being (McGillivray, 2005). The central indicators of economic well-being are income inequality, poverty and consumption (Osberg and Sharpe, 2002).

A number of official well-being indices can offer guidance on designing well-being measures at the regional level. The UN's Human Development Index (HDI), for instance, operationalizes the health dimension, standard of living and a knowledge dimension, while the OECD's Better Life Index enumerates eight dimensions of well-being – health, education, employment and the quality of working life, leisure, public services, physical environment, social environment and personal safety. The Index of Economic Well-being developed by the Centre for the Study of Living Standards comprises per capita consumption, wealth, economic inequality and economic security (Osberg and Sharpe, 2002).

The complexity of the socio-economic context of promoting well-being means that a single metric cannot adequately capture well-being (Stiglitz et al, 2018). The task requires consideration of a range of factors. This insight also guides the *OECD Regions at a Glance 2016* report (OECD, 2016), which presents the outputs from a wide-ranging database of subnational well-being indicators. Other measures have been developed by initiatives such as the *World Happiness Report*, which incorporates an array of dimensions of well-being (Helliwell et al, 2020). Such reports, however, share two main shortcomings: first, regional indicators for Europe are by and large only available for a short time span since the 2000s; and, second, measurement approaches tend to be broad and not theoretically motivated.

Chapter Three developed a theory of supranational spending and regional well-being that I use later in this chapter to operationalize well-being. I defined regional well-being as distributive justice in regions which promotes individual capabilities to achieve a good quality of life. In line with this approach, I propose to measure distributive justice and capabilities based on the contextual conditions that they can be expected to foster. Before discussing the results of these measurements, I describe how the data was collected.

There are two optimal sources for coding indicators of regional well-being: the various sources of regionally representative household panel data on income, from which measures of poverty and inequality can be calculated, and official statistics on unemployment, health, education and social inclusion. Data on poverty and income inequality can be obtained from the EU Statistics on Income and Living Conditions (EU-SILC) and its forerunner, the European Community Household Panel (ECHP). These annual statistics are designed to provide a comparable measure of income and standards of living in all participating EU member states. The overarching aim of this cross-national dataset is to help to equalize living conditions in the EU through the open method of coordination (Frick and Krell, 2011).

The ECHP contains panel data on individuals and households for 15 EU member states in 8 available data collection waves for the period 1994–2001. The underlying questionnaires are similar and the procedures for collecting information were coordinated by Eurostat. To extend the analytical foundation of this inquiry, the EU-SILC provides information on a wider sample of European countries (the 28 EU member states plus Iceland, Norway and Switzerland). I analyse seven waves available for this sample (2003–13). The ECHP and the EU-SILC do not uniformly report regional identifiers for the NUTS levels that would be appropriate for this study, however, and not all regions are consistently included at the same NUTS level over time. Nonetheless, despite these limitations, I was able to gather data for 189 NUTS regions in 16 countries.[1]

These household panels still represent the best available data sources for drawing inter-regional comparisons over time. Alternative sources, such as cross-national survey data on income from the European Social Survey, are less inclusive both regionally and temporally.

The data rely on the longitudinal components of the ECHP and the EU-SILC. In the EU-SILC, which is a rotating panel study for which households are interviewed in each of four consecutive years, my data are derived from the longitudinal component.[2] I combined the different ECHP and EU-SILC data files to create a Regional Well-Being Dataset that includes regional-level measures based on observations from individuals nested in households, using the corresponding person and household weights required to create social and economic indicators. To conduct inter-regional comparisons, I matched individual and regional identifiers across datasets to ensure that they identify cases distinctly (cf Mack and Lange, 2015; Mack, 2016).

As with all datasets, the ECHP and EU-SILC data have both strengths and weaknesses. Two caveats apply. First, deviations are known to exist from national household surveys in terms of sample structure (Frick and Krell, 2011). I therefore follow standard practice and create regional averages of well-being measures based on weighted equivalent household income (see Appendix C). Second, the sample size can be small for some NUTS 2 regions. In only 7 regions is the sample size below 100 observations, however, which means that this should not be an issue here.[3]

Ultimately, these household datasets provide crucial advantages that make it possible to ascertain patterns of well-being at a much more granular level than past alternatives. They are the most comparable measures across regions within different EU member states and over time.

Measuring regional well-being

Before mapping distributive justice and capabilities indicators, I briefly present the operationalization of these indicators. The creation of measures, their mathematical specification and their associated weightings are discussed in more detail in Appendix C.

Distributive justice

Distributive justice, as it is conceptualized in this book, requires that those in political office should endeavour to reduce inequalities in ways that maximize the welfare of society's most disadvantaged. I create a number of indicators of poverty and income inequality that are sensitive to changes in different aspects of intra-regional income distribution. This allows nuanced conclusions to be drawn regarding the possible effects of EU funding on inequality (Table 4.1).

The measures of relative income presented later have been created based on the absolute income measure of so-called net equivalized household income, which is a proxy for consumption in that it expresses the income that households have at their disposal (OECD, 2018). I create this measure from the ECHP/EU-SILC surveys in line with Eurostat's methodology by calculating the total income of a household after social transfers and taxes, along with any other deductions available for spending or saving, divided by the number of household members converted into a number of equivalized adults. Total income comprises: income from wages and salaries, as well as self-employment; income from real property; cash transfers from the government minus taxes; and household social security payments received. In order to code measures of relative income, I demarcated the poverty line at 60 per cent of national median income, calculated separately for each EU member state and year in order to factor in overall increases in living standards.

The first set of measures, to capture poverty, are part of the so-called Foster-Greer-Thorbecke (FGT) measurement family (Foster et al, 1984). These measures capture material deprivation and are to varying degrees sensitive to 'poverty gaps'. The 'head count ratio' demarcates the proportion of people below the poverty line, and by implication counts each individual in the same way. The poverty gap index captures the distance between poor people's standard of living and the poverty line, expressed as a ratio to the poverty line. The 'squared poverty gap index' denotes the weighted sum of all poverty gaps and assigns more weight to the poorest among the poor. It is calculated by averaging the squares of the poverty gaps relative to the poverty line. The higher the values on the measures, the greater the level of poverty. The squared poverty gap index is the most useful here as it weights the poorest among the poor more than the other measures; it is therefore used as the main measure of poverty in the explanatory analyses in Chapter Five.

Next, I created a set of income inequality measures. The first indicator in the set is widely used and cited in the political economy literature: the Gini coefficient. Gini ranges from 0 (complete equality) to 1 (complete inequality) and captures the extent to which income distribution within a regional economy deviates from perfect equality. Interestingly, World Bank data show that Gini indices at the national level ranged from about 0.3 to 0.6 worldwide during the period studied, while the regional Gini coefficient in my dataset ranged from about 0.2 to 0.55.

The Gini coefficient is sensitive to income differences at the middle (or mode) of the income distribution, which explains in part why otherwise different regions can have similar Gini coefficients. Gini may not put enough weight on important changes between the top and bottom earners or on income inequalities among the poor to capture well-being effectively (cf Jenkins, 2009; Piketty, 2014). I therefore calculated several additional measures of income inequality, which are also used in the explanatory analyses in Chapter Five.

The first is the family of so-called Generalized Entropy (GE) measures, which like the Gini coefficient vary between 0 (complete equality) and 1 (complete inequality). Originally promulgated as measures of randomness, and quite complex at that, they are commonly applied to income distribution in the context of inequality research. There are three useful measures of the degree of fairness in an income distribution

(Venkatasumbramanian et al, 2015): (i) the 'mean logarithmic deviation', which is relatively sensitive to changes at the bottom of the distribution; (ii) the 'Theil index', which captures variations similar to the Gini coefficient; and (iii) the 'squared coefficient of variation', which is relatively sensitive to changes at the top and thus differs more from the Gini.

The next group of measures are ratios, which express the income share of the wealthy as a multiple of that of the poor. I use the interdecile ratio P90/10 – that is, the decile ratio between the ninth and the first decile – which compares income in the highest income decile to that in the lowest. The P90/10 ratio is most sensitive to inequalities in relatively unequal societies and therefore overlaps with, but nonetheless complements, the Gini and GE measures. It shows best the share of economic wealth that goes to the economic elites compared with the poorest (cf Piketty, 2014). The interdecile ratio P90/50, which compares income in the top decile to the bottom half of the income distribution, correlates with Gini to a greater extent because it captures changes in the middle of the income distribution. I therefore use P90/10 in the statistical analyses in Chapter Five. Lower values in the P90/10 ratio indicate that low-income groups have achieved gains in income relative to high-income groups.[4]

Capabilities

To capture individual capabilities to achieve well-being aggregated at the regional level, I used several indicators (Table 4.1). To begin with, I used Eurostat data on the employment to working-age population ratio, or *employment per capita*, and rates of *unemployment* as proxies for access to employment. Both measures capture different phenomena, and are moderately correlated (r=-0.642, N=2,605). Next, I included a *youth inactivity* rate from Eurostat. This measure is relevant to the measurement of well-being, as the prospects for labour market success for those people who are unemployed

immediately following the end of their formal education, and who are seeking neither further education nor employment, are significantly reduced. Inactivity can lead to social exclusion and induce feelings of shame, rejection, anxiety and depression in young people (Albaek et al, 2015) and more generally (Atkinson et al, 2002).[5]

To demonstrate capabilities to achieve good health, I included two measures: *infant mortality* and *self-reported health* aggregated at the regional level. Other measures disaggregated at the regional level, such as the number of hospital beds or doctors per capita, are available from Eurostat, but these can often vary for organizational reasons, thereby yielding measures of institutional structures rather than outcomes. Infant mortality is typically used in welfare economics as a proxy for well-being (Kakwani et al, 2015). Related, previous studies have found that infant mortality is correlated with a lack of policy responsiveness to the well-being needs of vulnerable populations at both the local (Sampson, 2003) and the national (Kim and Saada, 2013) level.

The second measure of health incorporated here is self-perceptions of health. This measure was proposed by the World Health Organization (WHO) (De Bruin et al, 1996) and was also included in the Minimum European Health Module (Robine et al, 2010). Statistical cross-validation analyses suggest that the EU-SILC performed well in generating this measure in comparison to other surveys (Croezen et al, 2016). Since this measure is derived from individual self-perceptions and is therefore susceptible to bias, it has been subjected to multiple tests of reliability and validity. The reliability of self-perceived measures has been found to be as good as or better than alternative measures such as functional ability, chronic disease and psychological well-being (Lundberg and Manderbacka, 1996). Similarly, self-perception of health is strongly correlated with the results of tests using more extensive health scales, such as the Perceived Well-Being Scale (O'Brien Cousins, 1997), and a number of sub-scales of the 36-item Short Form Health

Survey (Brazier et al, 1992), which indicates a high degree of construct validity.

Table 4.1 summarizes the main well-being indicators used in the regression analyses of the determinants of well-being in Chapter Five and Chapter Six. To probe the validity of the well-being indicators, I used a common method for choosing indicators of well-being: I checked for correlations between well-being indicators and GDP (Kakwani et al, 2015). This showed that well-being indicators and GDP are either not or only weakly correlated throughout the time period observed, underlining their added value in terms of capturing distinct well-being phenomena. The other well-being indicators are used for the purposes of the descriptive analysis and to serve as robustness checks for the analyses in Chapter Five.

Mapping regional well-being

Global economic development provides important background for understanding well-being trajectories across poor and rich regions. After the 2001 dot-com crash, the world witnessed strong economic growth throughout the EU before the 2007–08 financial crisis, in part as a consequence of high levels of foreign direct investment, easy access to credit and low interest rates (European Economic Advisory Group, 2012). It is no surprise that Europe's regions saw strong economic growth in the early 2000s until the subprime mortgage crisis of 2008 hit the world economy. However, my analysis suggests that growth in the 2000s did not diminish the socio-economic divide within the EU.

The analysis here is based on an evaluation of changes in well-being indicators in the period 1994–2013, and a statistical assessment of how confident we can be that the observed differences in average regional well-being between rich and poor regions actually exist and are not due to measurement errors. The detailed measures can be found in Appendix Tables D.1 and D.2.[6]

Table 4.1: Measures of regional well-being

Indicator	Well-being dimensions captured	Correlation with GDP
	Capabilities	
Employment	Employment per capita, calculated as the proportion of employed persons aged 15 to 74 in the total regional population.	*r*=0.233, *N*=2,329
Unemployment	Unemployment rates, representing unemployed persons aged 15 to 74 as a percentage of the labour force, meaning the total number of people employed and unemployed including people actively seeking employment but excluding, for example, students and stay-at-home parents.	*r*=-0.166, *N*=2,765
Youth inactivity	Young people (aged 15 to 24) not in employment, education or training, as a percentage of the total cohort population, excluding survey respondents who did not answer the question.	*r*=-0.174, *N*=1,040
Infant mortality	Infant Mortality Rate (deaths of children under the age of one per 1,000 live births).	*r*=-0.146, *N*=2,622
Self-perceived health	Percentage of total regional population identifying health as good or very good in answer to the question: 'How is your health in general? Very good; good; fair; bad; very bad'.	*r*=0.084, *N*=915

(continued)

Table 4.1: Measures of regional well-being (continued)

Indicator	Well-being dimensions captured	Correlation with GDP
	Distributive justice	
FGT (α=2): Squared poverty gap index	Average squared normalized poverty gap index. Sensitive to inequalities among the poorest.	*r*=-0.129, *N*=819
Gini	Gini coefficient. Comparatively sensitive to changes in the middle part of the income distribution and around the mode.	*r*=0.195, *N*=758
GE (α=1): Theil index	Theil index. Comparatively sensitive to changes in the middle part of the income distribution.	*r*=0.179, *N*=813
GE (α=2): Squared coefficient of variation	Squared coefficient of variation. Comparatively sensitive to changes in the top part of the income distribution.	*r*=0.162, *N*=813
P90/10	Percentile ratio between the ninth and the first decile. Comparatively sensitive to changes in the bottom and top parts of the income distribution.	*r*=0.041, *N*=811

Notes: Pearson's correlation coefficient (*r*). The indicator used is GDP per capita in purchasing power parity. See Appendix C for more detailed coding descriptions and mathematical formulae.

Life tends to be better in rich regions

Two important aspects of the complex patterns of well-being since the early 1990s stand out. The first is that richer regions tend to perform better on all well-being indicators, with the

Figure 4.1: Regional unemployment rates

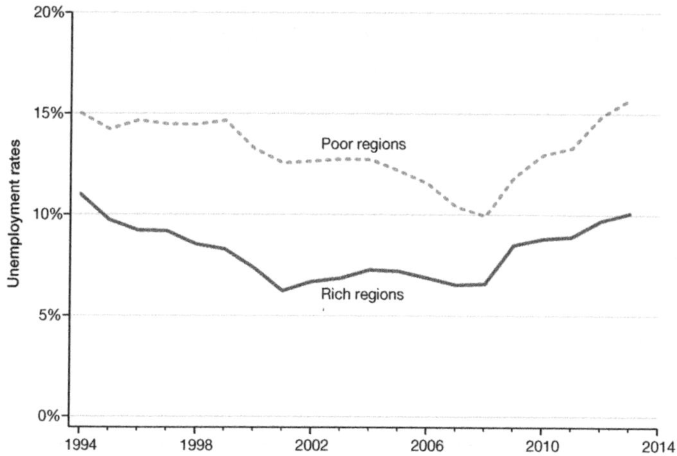

Notes: Unemployment rates (see Table 4.1)
Source: Eurostat

exception that rich regions face consistently higher levels of relative poverty. During the long-term budget 1994–99, for example, poorer regions were characterized, on average, by roughly 15 per cent unemployment, and about 15 per cent of the regional population was living below the poverty line. By contrast, richer regions saw about 9 per cent unemployment, and close to 23 per cent were living below the poverty line.

By the period 2000–06, labour markets had somewhat improved in both rich and poor regions, but the gap between the two remained largely the same (Figure 4.1). As is discussed in greater detail later, poverty and inequality remained largely constant throughout these years of increasing economic prosperity (Figure 4.2). The picture is different when it comes to health, which was on average better during the period 2000–06 than during the 1990s. About 65 per cent defined their own health as either good or very good in the rich regions, in contrast to roughly 61 per cent in the poor regions (see Figure 4.3).

Figure 4.2: Regional percentile ratio (90/10)

Notes: Percentile ratio 90/10 (see Table 4.1). Not calculated for 2013 due to too few observations in the high-income group in the EU-SILC.
Source: Author's regional well-being dataset

Figure 4.3: Self-perceived health

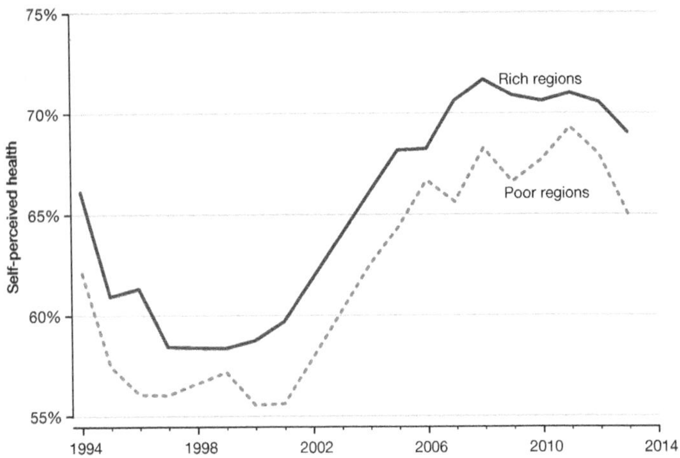

Notes: Percentage identifying health as good or very good (see Table 4.1)
Source: Author's regional well-being dataset

The global financial crisis fuelled a decline in living standards throughout Europe. In both wealthy and poor regions, during the period 2007–13, again unemployment was on average close to the average levels during the 2000–06 period, i.e., at about 13 per cent in poorer regions and 8 per cent in richer regions. Again, the gap between the two categories remained largely the same. However, unemployment during this period rose by more than 50 per cent, and levels of youth inactivity rose by almost 25 per cent. The percentage of people living below the poverty line was on average 15 per cent in poor and 18 per cent in rich regions. During the 2007–2013 period, the headcount ratio fell in rich regions but remained largely stable in poorer ones (Figure 4.4). Unsurprisingly, the increase in the number of those feeling in good or very good health came to a halt during the crisis years, during which both health indicators remained largely unchanged (Figure 4.3; Tables D.1 and D.2).

Poverty and inequality remain largely unchanged

Earnings inequalities were already rising steeply in Europe in the 1980s (European Commission, 2010d), and levels of poverty and income inequality have not significantly declined since the 1990s. More recent patterns of intra-country inequality, both in terms of the Gini coefficient, and the P90/10 ratio, are further evidence for the poverty and inequality standstill in Europe (Eurostat, 2020).

The rich regions in my sample have faced more serious problems linked to relative poverty and inequality to begin with in the 1990s, most likely linked to the urban poor. Rural regions tend to have lower levels of productivity but greater levels of equality and therefore less relative poverty and slightly fewer outright poor people. For instance, the Gini coefficient was slightly higher in richer regions throughout the 1990s (Gini=0.30) and in the 2000s before the crisis (Gini=0.29) than in poorer regions (Gini=0.27 and 0.26, respectively). During the crisis years of 2007–12, the average Gini coefficient was at 0.28 in both types of region. However, the analysis might show differences in inequality if it were to include a larger number of Eastern European member states, such as Bulgaria and Romania, which suffer from severe poverty in their rural populations.

That said, patterns of well-being *during* specific periods exhibit greater complexity. There were more notable changes in well-being during the 1990s in richer than in poorer regions. Unemployment, for example, fell by almost 25 per cent in the richer regions but only by about 2 per cent in the poorer ones (see Figure 4.1). However, the distributive justice indicators improved at similar rates in rich and poor regions (see Figures 4.2 to 4.4). There were weak changes in the Gini coefficient. Changes in the head count ratio and other indicators sensitive to income change among the poorest were more pronounced, suggesting that the situation of the poorest has improved since the 1990s.

Figure 4.4: Poverty

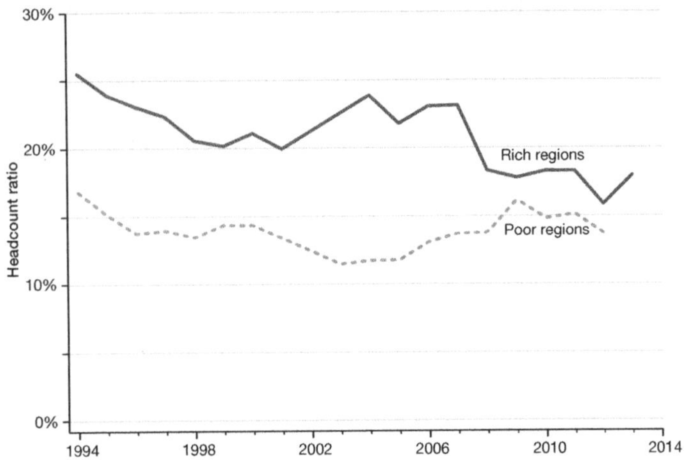

Notes: Head count ratio (see Table 4.1)
Source: Author's Regional Well-Being Dataset

By contrast, the period 2000–06 is characterized by an overall 'poverty standstill' (see also Cantillon, 2011). In addition, changes in the head count ratio and P90/10 suggest that problems arose far more in richer regions: during the 2000s, the rich in the rich regions became relatively more wealthy than the poor at a much faster pace than in the poor regions. Nonetheless, economic growth did not help to alleviate poverty and inequality in the poorer regions either. Particularly in southern Europe, the rapid economic growth of the 2000s inflated wages and prices, which helped to deepen the income imbalances in the poorer regions.

Moreover, the income gap between the richest and the poorest in society was similar in both types of regions in the 1990s and then again during the crisis years: the top 10 per cent earned roughly four times as much income as the bottom 10 per cent, and about twice as much as the median earner. The rich regions were able to alleviate the situation of the poor somewhat, while the situation of the poor in the poor regions remained largely unchanged. More recently, country indicators from 2018 suggest that life was getting better in the EU in terms of labour market outcomes before the outbreak of the COVID-19 pandemic. However, poverty and income inequality are persistent problems (OECD, 2020a) that will likely be exacerbated during periods of economic downturn and lockdown during the ongoing pandemic (European Economic Advisory Group, 2021).

As the UK left the EU in January 2020, it is interesting to highlight trends in the UK, where the populist anti-EU messages of missed economic opportunities (and immigration) certainly made the campaign to leave more effective (Hobolt, 2016). In the post-crash years after 2008, it was striking that London exhibited markedly different behaviour from the other regions of the UK. Income inequality in London varied relatively strongly in the 2000s, when an already relatively high Gini coefficient climbed as high as 55 in 2007 and then fell to 44 in 2011. Comparing the UK to France, another economically powerful European state, Paris is much more equal. The Gini coefficient of Île-de-France, which includes Paris, remained around 30 throughout the 1990s and the 2000s (see Appendix, Tables D.3 and D.4). In a wider European comparison, London suffers from much higher income inequality than other capital cities in Europe.[7]

In sum, poverty and inequality are persistent problems across both rich and poor regions. It is clear that in the countries observed, the rich regions on average do not tend to perform better than other regions in terms of tackling poverty and inequality. Again, this conclusion might have been different if Bulgaria and Romania had been included, where poverty rates tend to be higher in poorer rural areas, whereas poverty rates are higher in richer urban areas in Western Europe (Eurostat, 2020). Taken together, these findings underscore previous calls for greater attention to be paid to the issue of income inequality in the European public debate (see Beckfield, 2006; Busemeyer, 2014; Busemeyer and Tober, 2015; Castells-Quintana et al, 2015).

Conclusion

A fundamental challenge in the study of regional development is the lack of consistent and comprehensive datasets on well-being. In contrast to existing well-being databases at the subnational level, the dataset compiled for this book is more inclusive in terms of its coverage of the 1990s and its inclusion of a number of poverty and inequality indicators well-suited to capturing the different shades of well-being. The results underscore that it is essential to look beyond GDP in order to fully comprehend the condition of Europe's poor and otherwise disadvantaged.

Two dynamics in regional well-being are worth reiterating. First, in terms of *levels* of well-being, life is better in rich regions. Rich regions tend to perform better on well-being than poor regions, with regard to wealth, labour market conditions, prospects for young people, infant mortality and improved public health. By January 2020, labour market performance was largely back to pre-2008 crisis levels but the gap between rich and poor regions remained. Second, in terms of *changes* in well-being, poverty and income inequality are structural problems that have not changed significantly for the better since 1994.

It is tempting to use these findings to forecast the likely impacts on well-being of the current economic downturn. In general, crises are known to negatively affect people's health, for reasons linked to poverty, social exclusion, social inactivity and financial strain (European Economic Advisory Group, 2021: Karanikolos et al, 2015). However, it is not the goal of this book to make predictions, but rather to use the descriptive findings to set the stage for the ensuing analysis in Chapter Five and Chapter Six of when and why EU social investment, among a range of other factors, shapes regional well-being.

FIVE

EU Spending Effects on Regional Well-Being

This chapter explores a central argument of this book: that EU social investments will enhance well-being if they improve the capabilities of poor and otherwise disadvantaged people. Under the current legal framework and given domestic funding practices, however, positive well-being effects are only likely in rich regions.* Rich areas typically constitute the powerful urban centres around which most wealth has historically accumulated. Much of the inequality in the EU has resulted from the richest people and places pulling away from more rural parts of a region (Collier, 2018). The richer areas tend to have a more skilled regional workforce and better-functioning institutions (Charron, 2016), and their relatively high stock of human and social capital makes them attractive project partners for governments.

In this chapter, I show that this dynamic tends to work to the benefit of labour markets but works to the detriment of distributive justice. That EU funding of human capital can have positive effects on employment is known (Coelho, 2019; Mohl, 2016), but it is not sufficiently recognized that people in poor regions typically cannot take advantage of the related employment growth. Drawing on the Regional Well-Being Dataset introduced in Chapter Four, this chapter shows that

* My thanks to Ognjen Zugic for his valuable contributions to this chapter.

EU social investments have positive effects on employment growth and unemployment, but that these effects are small and only hold in rich regions. Moreover, I find no robust effects of EU social investments on youth activity, infant mortality and self-reported health; adverse effects are found on income inequality in poor regions.

In the remainder of this chapter, I lay out how I will quantitatively examine the effects of EU social investments on regional well-being indicators, present the results and discuss the evidence against the backdrop of previous research. I do so for the capability indicators first and then for the distributive justice indicators. The chapter concludes by linking the analysis in this chapter to the qualitative inquiry on these effects in Chapter Six, which will make sense of the statistical results by drawing on official documents, news media and interview evidence.

Estimating capabilities: research design

The best approach to estimating the likely effects of EU funding on well-being at the regional level is by way of regression analysis.[1] Such analyses, if carefully done, can yield reliable estimates of EU funding effects. My aim is to provide estimates that take account of the fact that EU funding effects may occur following time lags and are likely to be related to other regional and national contexts and conditions in complex ways.

Measuring capabilities

The first part of the analysis uses the five main capability indicators that were introduced in Chapter Four as dependent variables: unemployment, employment, youth inactivity, infant mortality and self-perceptions of health. This section discusses how the potential determinants of these five indicators, respectively, were measured.

Measuring EU funding

First, I operationalised the main explanatory factors of interest: EU social and economic investments (see Chapter One and Appendix B). EU spending measures were adjusted for inflation to enable cross-time comparisons, as real spending can be evaluated differently depending on economic developments, specifically prices. I used the logarithm of these measures in the analyses to prevent any outlier regions that receive extremely high levels of funding from biasing the estimates. For example, only four regions receive more than €90 per capita in social investments – Bremen, Hainaut, Madeira and Réunion – while about two thirds of regions receive less than €10 per capita.

I incorporated measures of EU social investment lagged by one and two years to adjust for potential short-term effects.[2] In other words, each of the models includes two lagged social spending variables: one that expresses spending in the previous year and the other an expression of spending two years before the dependent variable was measured. This takes account of the fact that spending can have delayed effects on poverty and inequality outcomes.

The dataset compiled for this study comprises annual funding data for the same regions. This approach has major advantages as it makes it possible to examine the effects of actual rather than earmarked spending, as used in most previous studies on EU regional funding, and to consider the potential endogeneity issues that may arise due to reverse causality, omitted variable bias or joint determination of the dependent and one or several independent variables (simultaneity).

I tested for evidence to support my hypothesis that economic funds have no positive effect on well-being outcomes. This allowed me to ascertain whether economic investments are indeed less useful than social investments when it comes to enhancing regional well-being. Economic funds are typically spent on major economic projects, many of which entail the construction of physical infrastructure, the development of telecommunications and energy resources and increased investment in businesses. It is my contention that social investments are more clearly connected to improvements in well-being indicators, since this is the category expressly tasked with making such interventions.

Measuring regional context factors shaping capabilities

To estimate EU social funding effects in rich and poor regions separately, a dichotomous variable was created that equals 1 if a region has Objective 1 or Convergence status, and 0 if it does not. Chapter Three shows that there are compelling reasons to expect EU social investments to have no effects in regions eligible under the Objective 1 or the Convergence objective, which struggle with a GDP below 75 per cent of the EU average and are beset with the ramifications of structural decline, as they may lack the human and social capital to use EU funds successfully.

Modelling labour market and youth-related outcomes requires a decision on whether to add indicators for institutions and investment as potential explanatory factors of these outcomes. The substantial literature on macro-economic developments in economic activity and unemployment provides useful insights on modelling choices. Economic activity and employment are among the most-studied phenomena in economics, but there is no consensus around the predictors of employment (Acemoglu, 2009). Institutional theories typically highlight labour market institutions, such as trade union density, labour market regulation and taxation, as potential sources of wage and price formation, but the evidence is mixed (Hegelund and Taalbi, 2019).

For this reason, I chose a 'conservative' modelling approach and omitted investment measures from the labour market and youth models to avoid overspecification. Robustness checks confirm that the main results are robust when controlling for domestic education investment in these models (see the online

appendix). In addition, based on the literature cited earlier, which treats union density as a standard control in models of unemployment (Stockhammer et al, 2014), I included *union density* as a variable, measured as the ratio of wage and salary earners that are members of trade unions divided by the total number of wage and salary earners (OECD, 2019).

The models also incorporate growth in both GDP per capita and population density. I controlled for economic growth lagged by one year in all models to allow for any shocks to the regional economy that might negatively affect well-being outcomes. Here, economic growth lagged by one year is included in all models, as Chapter Four has illustrated that some regions demonstrated short-term idiosyncrasies in well-being developments that could be due to external economic shocks.[3]

Regional population and area data are used to compute population density as the population divided by the total area of a region in square kilometres. Regions with a relatively high population density often have a heterogeneous population in terms of social and economic activity. Previous research suggests that richer metropolitan areas in the EU are slightly more economically unequal than rural areas and other urban areas (Boulant et al, 2016; OECD, 2018). In line with this observation, theories of technology uptake would predict that population density undermines well-being outcomes because it is an indicator of technology uptake, which increases returns to highly skilled people and the industries in which they work, thereby exacerbating income inequality at a higher rate in richer than in rural, often poorer, regions.

The infant mortality and health models, like the labour market models, also include GDP per capita growth and population density as explanatory variables. Generally, economic development improves healthcare provision and better health outcomes might be expected in such areas, as indicated in the descriptive analysis of health outcomes in richer versus poorer regions in Chapter Four. In densely populated areas, health outcomes may be higher given that urbanized centres typically have higher skilled and wealthier populations (Bertinelli and Zou, 2008). Given strong evidence that health spending improves services and therefore health outcomes (WHO, 2018), health spending was also added to the health models.

Quantitative data on capabilities could be collected for 16 EU member states: Austria, Belgium, the Czech Republic, Finland, France, Germany, Greece, Hungary, Ireland, Italy, the Netherlands, Poland, Portugal, Spain, Sweden and the UK. States from all geographical areas were included to capture trends from the eastern, northern, southern and western parts of the EU.

In sum, using these data, I ran five models, using one capability indicator at a time as a dependent variable (Table 5.1). I repeated the estimation for each model using data from poor regions only, and then using data from rich regions only, thereby testing if the drivers of regional well-being differ across types of regions. Appendix E elaborates on the mathematical formulae used to construct the five statistical models and reports the regression results in detail. The online appendix describes an array of robustness checks addressing potential endogeneity and testing alternative model specifications.

Weak EU spending effects on capabilities

The results can be interpreted as the effects of EU investment and other factors on capability indicators *within* regions over time. In what follows, I discuss only the effects that are consistent across a large number of robustness checks that test how sensitive EU social investment effects are to alternative modelling assumptions and specifications (see the online appendix). In essence, EU social investments were found to influence the regional outcomes of a range of well-being indicators linked to employment and unemployment– – but only in the rich regions. By contrast, there was no robust evidence that social investments affect youth- or health-related outcomes.[4]

Table 5.1: Regression analysis: EU social investment effects on capabilities

	(1)	(2)	(3)	(4)	(5)
	Unemployment	**Employment**	**Youth inactivity**	**Infant mortality**	**Self-perceived health**
EU social investments (log) (*t-1*)	Included	Included	Included	Included	Included
EU social investments (log) (*t-2*)	Included	Included	Included	Included	Included
Population density (log)	Included	Included	Included	Included	Included
GDP growth (*t-1*)	Included	Included	Included	Included	Included
Union density (*t-1*)	Included	Included	Included	–	–
National health spending (*t-1*)	–	–	–	Included	Included
Number of observations	1,746	1,793	1,566	1,799	669
Number of rich regions	102	103	99	90	58
Number of poor regions	71	71	66	65	34

Notes: *t-1* indicates a one-year lag, *t-2* a two-year lag. Longer lags were not found to matter in a consistent way. These models are two-way panel data regression models with annual fixed effects included in each model and Driscoll-Kraay standard errors that are robust to general forms of spatial and temporal dependence (clustered at the level of regions). Given their skewed nature, some indicators were logarithmized, implying that they are closer to being normally distributed.

These results are summarized in Table 5.2. Few desired effects of EU social investments on unemployment and employment are found, which I illustrate in Figures 5.1 and 5.2.[5] Social investment effects are shown with their respective 95 confidence intervals, which indicate how likely it is that the effect is due to measurement error or chance. Where these overlap with the horizontal zero line, the possibility cannot be excluded that the effect is not genuine. Figure 5.1 illustrates that EU social investments lagged by two years lead to decreases in unemployment rates in the full sample and in rich regions. Investments lagged by two years are more often significant than investments lagged by one year, indicating that one year is too short to detect effects.

More specifically, the results suggest that doubling EU social funding per capita in rich regions would lead to a roughly 0.4 percentage point decrease in the rate of unemployment 2 years after the investment, given the statistical model.[6] By way of illustration, in Scotland, a region of the UK with approximately the average GDP per capita of the EU, if EU social investment had doubled in 2011, this would have resulted in a 0.4 percentage point decrease in unemployment from 7.2 to 6.8 per cent in 2013. This would mean around 15,000 people taken out of unemployment.[7] Poorer regions would have been unlikely to benefit from increased funding in terms of lower unemployment rates – an issue to which I will return in Chapter Six.

Figure 5.2 illustrates funding effects on employment. Considering that employment is less volatile over time than unemployment rates, it is all the more striking that despite the small amounts of EU social funding involved, there are discernible effects in the full sample and in rich regions. To be sure, these effects are very small. Doubling EU social investments per capita would lead to an only 0.5 per cent increase in employment per capita. In the example of Scotland in 2013, doubling EU social funding would have increased employment from 46 per cent to about 46.2 per cent.[8]

Table 5.2: Regression results: EU social investment effects on capabilities

	All regions		Rich regions		Poor regions	
	t-1	*t-2*	*t-1*	*t-2*	*t-1*	*t-2*
Unemployment	Desired effect (–)	Desired effect (–)	No effect	Desired effect (–)	Mixed evidence	No effect
Employment	No effect	Desired effect (+)	No effect	Desired effect (+)	No effect	No effect
Youth inactivity	Mixed evidence	Mixed evidence	No effect	Mixed evidence	No effect	No effect
Infant mortality	No effect	No effect	No effect	No effect	No effect	No effect
Self-perceived health	No effect	Mixed evidence	No effect	No effect	No effect	Mixed evidence

Notes: *t-1* indicates a one-year lag, *t-2* a two-year lag. Results are based on analyses reported in Appendix Tables E.1–E.3.

Figure 5.1: Effects of EU social investments on unemployment rates

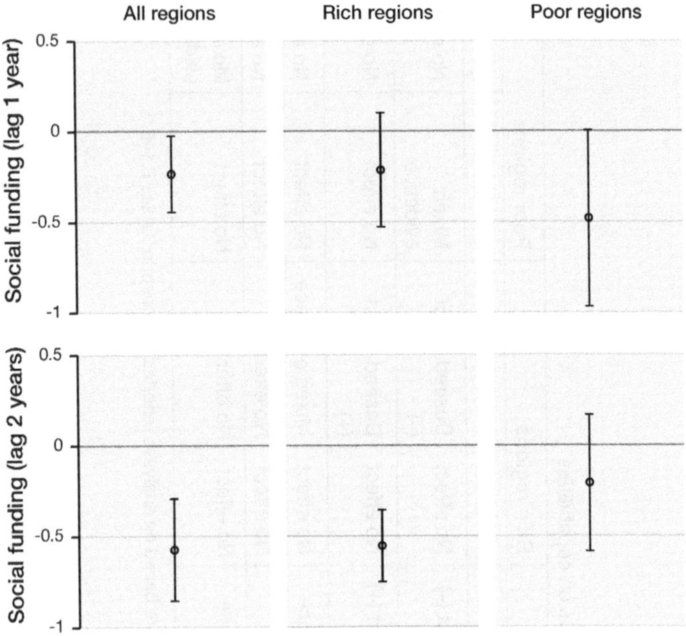

GDP growth is an important factor in all the alternative explananda. First and foremost, the effects of growth on unemployment and employment rates are greater than the social investment effects discussed. Moreover, growth fosters youth activity and improves self-perceptions of health in the poor regions. In terms of the determinants of health-related outcomes, population density is positively associated with self-perceived health in poor regions, indicating that public health is better in urban centres with relatively highly skilled inhabitants. Finally, national health spending is found to be associated with the health outcomes identified, which is in line with both previous research and policy guidelines (WHO, 2018). However, the effects are very small, potentially due to the relatively small variations in health in industrialized democracies when compared to developing countries.

Figure 5.2: Effects of EU social investments on employment per capita

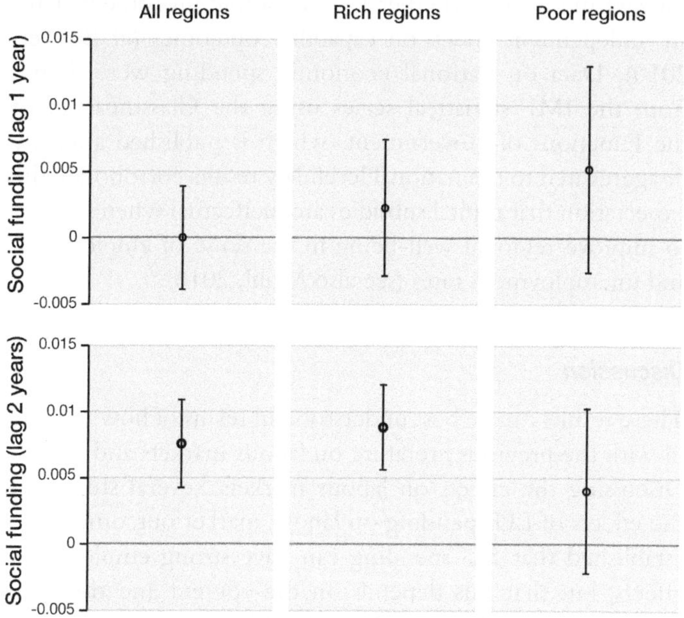

Notes: As in Figure 5.1, these are conditional marginal effects and 95 per cent confidence intervals from the two-way fixed effects panel regression models summarized in Table 5.1. Reported results that are significant at p<.05 are consistent across a large number of different model specifications and when accounting for potential endogeneity by using Generalized Method of Moments (GMM) estimation (Roodman, 2006).

Next, I examined whether similar effects of EU investments on capability indicators can be found in the context of economic investments. They are the EU's main tool for boosting productivity and thereby competitiveness, in the sense of traditional regional development policy to reduce *inter*-regional disparities. In the models of the effects of economic investment on capability indicators, I controlled for national economic spending as a proportion of GDP, which includes such categories as general economic and commercial affairs, research and development, agriculture, forestry, energy, construction, transport, tourism, fishing and hunting. This allowed me to test whether EU economic investments have an 'independent effect' on capability outcomes (cf Bouvet, 2010). Data on national economic spending were drawn from the IMF statistical series using the Classification of the Functions of Government, which is published annually disaggregated to the national level. My results corroborate the expectation that capital subsidies are ineffectual when seeking to improve regional well-being in the sense of employment and unemployment rates (see also Mohl, 2016).[9]

Discussion

These results can be best understood in terms of how they tie in with the previous literature on labour markets and health. Discussing the effects on labour markets, several studies of the effects of EU spending on labour market outcomes have established that EU spending can have strong employment effects, but that this depends on the context and the time period studied. The basic idea is that EU funding has positive employment effects when productivity increases (Mohl, 2016). The existing literature finds positive employment effects from the ERDF for firms in northern and central Italy (Bondonio and Greenbaum, 2006). In addition, in a sample of eight EU member states covering the period 1975–99, Bouvet (2005) shows a positive effect of EU regional funding on employment growth. More recent evidence, however, is far less encouraging, observing no positive employment effects for EU member states (Heinemann et al, 2009) or regions (Becker et al, 2010). Research conducted by Becker et al (2013) indicates that Objective 1 funding does not crowd out but increases domestic investment, but identifies no effects of EU funding on employment or unemployment between 1989 and 2006.

Mohl and Hagen (2011) conducted a nuanced analysis of EU funding effects on employment. Investigating EU human capital investment and capital subsidies in areas with highly skilled and less skilled workforces, respectively, they found an EU funding effect on employment in the period 1999–2007 only in areas with highly skilled workers. The success of labour market measures such as training and career counselling appears indeed to be conditional on their effect on the existing stock of human capital. The evidence in this chapter ties in well with these results and exposes one of the signal deficiencies in the common belief in the utility of EU funding in promoting employment growth: while some people in rich regions might benefit from employment growth, a large proportion of the relevant population can experience negative impacts linked to increased inequalities, or no impact at all.

That the recent evidence for employment effects is mixed is striking given that EU funding since the 2000s has sought to mainstream social investment goals more and more. The ESF in particular has devoted most of its resources to labour market interventions since 1992, with project goals that are clearly traceable to the outcomes shown to benefit from funding. Training, education, flexibilization, direct job creation and career counselling constitute the core components of ESF funding, and a large part of the ESF's mission is to support young people. Since the early 2000s, the Lisbon goals have been promoted through various mainstreaming efforts to promote human capital investment at all stages of life (Chapter Two).

If the EU's growth and capacity-building motor – EU regional funding – is to enhance labour market outcomes, especially for vulnerable groups, reforms will be needed to foster such effects. Persisting with the traditional preoccupation with using funding to increase aggregate productivity – to the practical exclusion of other considerations, most notably well-being of the most vulnerable – merely sustains defective EU policies and domestic funding practices, as evidenced in the presence of employment effects in rich regions only.

Turning to public health, it is worth noting that this absence of funding effects on average public health does not mean that EU funding does not improve health care for some. For instance, previous case study literature has shown instances of healthcare improvements linked to the provision of basic services in some regions, especially the poorer ones, thanks to EU funding. For example, Bachtler et al (2013, p. 68) describe the case of Andalucia, where 'three new hospitals were built with the renovation of many others and also primary health centres. 103 new secondary schools and 34 primary schools were built, but also sports facilities such as 23 indoor pools and 18 sports centres as well as care centres and shelters for the homeless'.

That I do not find any effects on public health in the aggregate, as measured by self-reported health and infant mortality, may be due to the fact that the building of hospitals and health centres does not automatically translate into improved public health. Rather, such endeavours need to be understood within the context of different European health care systems, which vary in the extent of an array of aspects of public health, such as administrative efficiency, quality of care and financial protection of poor people in need of healthcare (Thomson et al, 2009). Future research could usefully quantify such more specific aspects of public health to further examine EU funding effects on health.

Estimating distributive justice: research design

The dependent variables – that is, the regional poverty and inequality outcomes which were introduced as measures of distributive justice in Chapter Four – are the squared poverty gap index, the Gini coefficient, the Theil index, the squared coefficient of variation and the 90/10 percentile ratio (P90/10). To estimate EU funding effects, I used the *social investments* and *economic investments* indicators described. Again, I included these measures lagged by one and two years to account for potential short-term effects.[10] As noted, I did not expect economic funds to shape well-being outcomes, but tested to see whether there is any evidence to support my hypothesis.

In this portion of the analysis, I again examine the effects of a number of contextual factors that might influence regional well-being independently from EU funding effects. Once again, I estimated the effects of EU social funding in rich and poor regions separately, using the dummy variable that equals 1 if a region has Objective 1/Convergence status and 0 if not. All the models use a measure of *population density* and *tertiary education*. The former was operationalized in the previous section. The latter is measured as a percentage of the total regional population for whom tertiary education is the highest level of education completed (cf Castells-Quintana et al, 2015). I also controlled for economic growth in all the models to verify whether shocks to the regional economy could have negatively affected well-being outcomes. Economic growth was lagged by one year, as Chapter Four found that some regions exhibit short-term idiosyncrasies in well-being developments likely linked to external economic shocks. Finally, I took account of the potentially confounding effects on well-being resulting from high or low levels of *national educational spending* as a proportion of GDP (cf Busemeyer, 2014).

Taken together, because the availability of data sources varies, the analysis in this section spans 11 states in different geographical areas of the EU with a combined population of more than 150 million: Belgium, the Czech Republic, Finland, France, Germany, Greece, Italy, Portugal, Spain and Sweden, as well as the UK, which was still an EU member state at the time. Table 5.3 summarizes which variables are included in the models that are described here (see also Appendix E).

EU spending harms distributive justice

The quantitative analysis explains the variations in well-being *within* regions over time. I present only the robust results,

Table 5.3: Regression analysis: EU social investment effects on distributive justice

	(1)	(2)	(3)	(4)	(5)
	Squared poverty gap index	**Gini**	**Theil index (log)**	**Squared coefficient of variation (log)**	**P90/10 (log)**
EU social investments (*t-1*)	Included	Included	Included	Included	Included
EU social investments (*t-2*)	Included	Included	Included	Included	Included
Population density	Included	Included	Included	Included	Included
GDP growth (*t-1*)	Included	Included	Included	Included	Included
Tertiary education (*t-1*)	Included	Included	Included	Included	Included
Nat. educational spending (*t-1*)	Included	Included	Included	Included	Included
Number of observations in total	543	544	544	544	542
Number of rich regions	57	57	57	57	57
Number of poor regions	34	34	34	34	34

Notes: *t-1* indicates a one-year lag, *t-2* a two-year lag. Deeper lags were not found to matter consistently. These models are two-way panel data regression models with annual fixed effects included in each model and Driscoll-Kraay standard errors that are robust to general forms of spatial and temporal dependence (clustered at the level of regions). Given their skewed nature, some indicators were logarithmized, implying that they are closer to being normally distributed.

which are summarized in Table 5.4 and depicted in Figures 5.3 and 5.4. Again, it is striking how few effects the analysis can establish.

The key finding is that EU social investments have no effect on poverty and inequality in rich regions but tend to exacerbate inequality in poor regions. The fact that no EU funding effect is visible from the pooled sample that includes all regions corroborates the argument that it is important to distinguish between poor and rich regions when analysing the socio-economic consequences of EU spending.[11]

More specifically, in poor regions, Figures 5.3 and 5.4 are demonstrative of an adverse effect of EU social spending on inequality, as the coefficients of the lagged spending variables by 1 and 2 years in the case of Gini, and by 1 year in the case of the squared coefficient of variation, are statistically significant at the 5 per cent level or higher. To illustrate, doubling EU

Table 5.4: Regression results: EU social investment effects on distributive justice

	All regions		Rich regions		Poor regions	
	t-1	*t-2*	*t-1*	*t-2*	*t-1*	*t-2*
Squared poverty gap index	No effect	No effect	No effect	Mixed evidence	Mixed evidence	No effect
Gini	No effect	No effect	No effect	No effect	Adverse effect (+)	Adverse effect (+)
Theil index	No effect	No effect	No effect	No effect	Mixed evidence	No effect
Squared coefficient of variation	No effect	No effect	No effect	No effect	Adverse effect (+)	No effect
P90/10	No effect	Mixed evidence	No effect	No effect	No effect	No effect

Notes: *t-1* indicates a one-year lag, *t-2* a two-year lag. Results are based on the analyses reported in Appendix Tables E.4–E.6.

Figure 5.3: Effects of EU social investments on the Gini coefficient

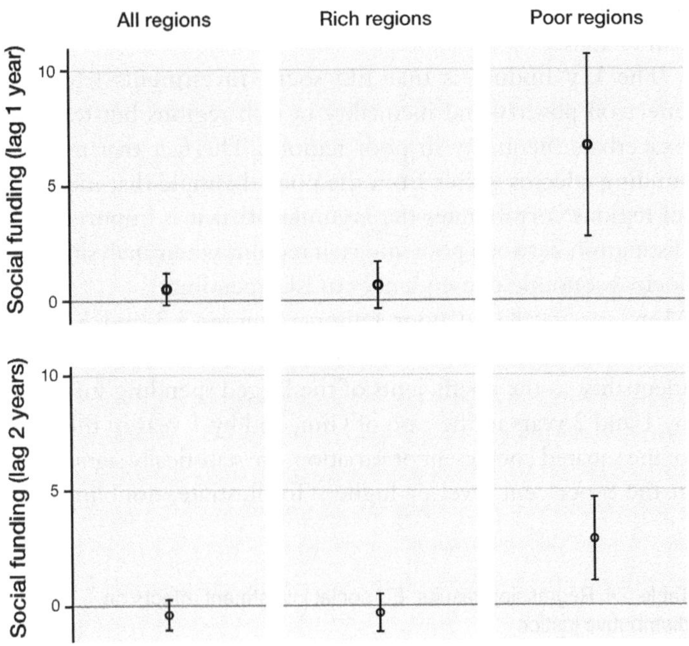

social spending, lagged by 1 year, is associated with an almost 4-point increase in the Gini coefficient,[12] and an about 44 per cent increase in the squared coefficient of variation.[13]

This suggests that EU social spending exacerbates inequality especially for those indicators that are sensitive to changes in the middle part of the income distribution (Gini) and in the top part (squared coefficient of variation). Interestingly, no effects were found on the 90/10 percentile ratio, suggesting that EU social investments do not affect the relationship between the bottom 10 per cent and the top 10 per cent of regional income distributions, but instead widen the middle of the income distribution between the 75th and the 25th percentiles.

I replicated all the models to estimate the effects of economic, rather than social, funding to ascertain whether capital subsidies

Figure 5.4: Effects of EU social investments on the squared coefficient of variation

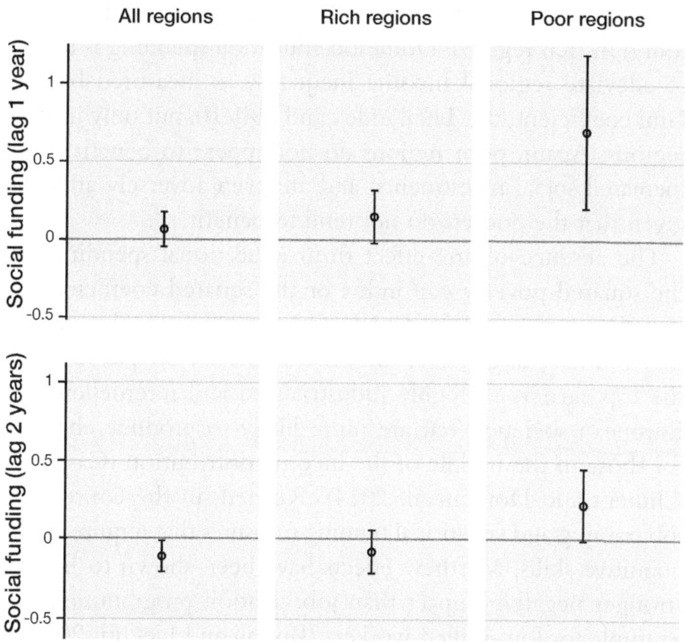

Notes: As in Figure 5.3, these are conditional marginal effects at 95 per cent confidence intervals from the two-way fixed effects panel regression models summarized in Table 5.2. Reported results that are significant at p<.05 are consistent across a large number of different model specifications and when accounting for potential endogeneity by using GMM estimation (Roodman, 2006).

that do not explicitly target human capital have any effect on well-being. As expected, however, I did not find any robust effects.[14]

In terms of the alternative explanations tested, other variables do have explanatory power. All the models contain a variable that keeps the skills levels of the workforce 'constant'. High skill levels among workers in regions have been shown to increase inequality within EU regions in terms of Gini and P90/10 (Castells-Quintana et al, 2015). By replicating this analysis, I also found this factor to exacerbate income inequality in poor regions when focusing on the Theil index and the squared coefficient of variation. However, these results are not found in rich regions. Domestic education spending is found to alleviate regional income inequality as measured by the Gini coefficient, the Theil index and P90/10, but only in rich regions. Again, poor regions do not appear to benefit from increased social investments, and are even adversely affected given that the poorest do not tend to benefit.

The absence of any effect from educational spending on the squared poverty gap index or the squared coefficient of variation can be explained by the fact that educational spending may not have large effects on the incomes of the poorest and the top earners in highly industrialized and interdependent European societies, but are more likely to produce changes for those in the middle of the income distribution (Castelló-Climent and Doménech, 2014). Related, in the context of job training and vocational training measures that require some cognitive skills, Matthew effects have been shown to have a stronger negative impact than job creation programmes, for example for low-skilled workers (Bonoli and Liechti, 2018).

Discussion

How good a fit are these results with previous broader explanations of inequality? The main focus of the inequality literature is on inequality trends across global regions and states, and on explaining inter-state variations in inequality. While the debate on the determinants of inequality is far from settled, it is possible to distinguish between two main arguments. The first is linked to market-based accounts of inequality and the second to institutional explanations. Institutional explanations are based on the assumption that market forces do not tell the full story of inequality. For example, it has been shown that the growth–income inequality relationship can be spurious when European integration (Beckfield, 2019), macro-sociological ideological influences (Mann and Riley, 2007), educational institutions (Busemeyer, 2014) or public sector investment (Pontusson, 2005) are taken into account.

Within this sizeable and burgeoning literature, one influential line of thinking views social investments over a person's lifetime, together with active labour market policies, as the major source of reduced income inequality. In part, this is because social investments can enhance human capital, and in part it is because growth alleviates fiscal pressures on indebted states, allowing them to invest more in the well-being of their citizens. Better-distributed education, especially, through its influence on human capital, has a positive effect on equality of income (Salverda et al, 2011). A link between education and reduced inequality can depend on the nature of the spending (Busemeyer, 2014). If greater education inputs are invested, especially in households with children and young people, this can enhance the skills of young people and people in the workforce more generally, with positive effects on alleviating inequality (OECD, 2014).

Taken together, the results suggest that EU social investments do not yield strong positive well-being effects. On the contrary, adverse well-being effects are found in poor regions, where groups of skilled people are able to capitalize on EU funding, further increasing income gaps.

Conclusion

The major findings of this portion of my analysis are twofold. First, EU social investments enhance two of the five capability indicators of well-being in rich regions, that is, the labour market-related well-being outcomes. No effects were found on the youth- and health-related indicators. In poorer regions, no well-being effects were detected for any of the indicators. Second, EU social investments tend to exacerbate income inequality in poor regions. I also examined whether the effects of EU social investment on regional well-being are greater than the effects of the EU's economic investment. However, the results suggest that EU economic investments have no effect at all on shaping regional well-being.

These findings are crucial. They suggest that EU spending helps the unemployed in rich regions but not vulnerable populations such as young people mired in inactivity who may require skills reorientation and other training. In the ensuing chapter, I will discuss these findings in depth, using qualitative material to identify several major barriers to EU social investment having an effect on well-being. Policy integration, amounts and targeting of social funding, information and capacity will be shown to be crucial to understanding why EU social funds have only weak – and sometimes adverse – effects on well-being. These are elaborated on further in Chapter Six.

SIX

Barriers to Improving Regional Well-Being

The analysis in Chapter Five has given EU social investments a mixed bill of health: EU social investments foster employment in rich regions, which should be unsurprising given the strong focus on improving education, training and employment prospects. However, young people, who have been a key focus of the ESF over almost 30 years and are one of the most vulnerable groups to social exclusion in society, do not appear to benefit. In addition, EU social investments are found to have adverse effects on income inequality in poor regions, for which EU regional funding is mainly intended, and where people face pervasive inequality and extensive loss of opportunities.

This chapter seeks to provide a deeper understanding of why EU spending fosters employment but harms distributive justice. It explores the argument developed in Chapter Three that richer regions are more likely to capitalize on the effects of EU social investment on well-being, due to their superior endowments of human and social capital compared to poor regions. Consistent support for skilled labour in wealthy areas within regions implies that the already better off benefit the most from social investments. Building on this argument, this chapter identifies five main barriers to obtaining well-being effects from EU social investments. These barriers were identified based on an inductive analysis of news media evidence gathered from the daily bulletins provided by Agence Europe, qualitative and standardized interviews with domestic and EU policymakers conducted during and in the aftermath of the 2007–12 crisis (see Appendix A), and insights from previous literature on EU regional and social policy (e.g., Pierson, 1996; Chalmers, 2013; Schraff, 2014).

In a nutshell, I show that regional and national authorities tend to select projects in ways that maximize their own interests, and that there are powerful structural barriers to providing these authorities with incentives to pursue EU social goals forcefully: (a) social and economic investments remain largely siloed; (b) social funding amounts continue to be small; (c) small amounts are spread thinly and to richer areas; (d) informational asymmetries persist; and (e) shortfalls in administrative capacity in poor regions undermine the ability of resource-poor actors to attract EU funding. I discuss each barrier in turn.

Social and economic investments remain siloed

It is neither news nor surprising that domestic practices in using EU funding do not systematically take social performance into consideration when budgeting, formulating OPs and selecting projects (e.g., Bachtler et al, 2019). That country-ownership to using EU funds has overall adverse effects on well-being in poor regions, however, is both. The continuing compartmentalization in silos of social and economic policies is a challenge to positive well-being effects of EU funding.

EU regional policy has traditionally targeted inter-regional disparities. The traditional understanding of regional policy as growth-enhancing investment to promote socio-economic equality between regions reflects a historical compromise that has enabled governments with vastly different interests to agree on a joint budget. This compromise reflects the lack of political will among governments to delegate power to the EU in the area of social policy (Pierson, 1996).

The member states' half-hearted commitment to EU goals contributes to the fact that project selection varies in terms of goals and quality across Europe, and that projects are usually selected to fit in previous growth-enhancing regional development policies.[1] Only a few member states explicitly emphasize social goals in their regional development policies, such as social exclusion (Finland), intra-regional disparities (Greece), socio-economic rebalancing (Italy) or enhanced polycentrism and inclusiveness (Ireland). In member states in which there is a constitutional guarantee to reduce inter-regional disparities, such as Germany, the focus on enhancing growth through productivity is especially strong. In such cases, 'equality in living standards' does not mean intra-regional equity, but inter-regional equity. Several other member states seek to achieve 'sustainable development' with their regional policies (Belgium, the Czech Republic, France, Hungary, Slovakia and Spain), but most focus is on increasing competitiveness and productivity with no consideration of social goals (OECD, 2010). Against this background, it comes as no surprise that only a small number of EU member states have emphasized the goal of social inclusion in their budgetary plans for EU-funded programmes in the period observed in this study (Bachtler et al, 2007; European Commission, 2014a).

Only slowly have *intra*-regional disparities been emphasized in the EU regional policy framework through increased social mainstreaming (Chapter Two). Even so, regional inequalities are still widely conceptualized as differences between regions. This is at odds with social goals pertaining to well-being, as analyses of inter-regional disparities alone mask the fact that EU funds regularly fail to benefit the neediest groups within regions, but instead often assist already skilled and powerful groups (see also De Rynck and McAleavey, 2001).

In the three-stage project selection process described in Chapter Two, consisting of 'programming', assigning responsibilities for project selection and then implementing co-financed projects, it is also insufficiently recognized that there are conflicting time horizons between the traditional regional development goal of enhancing growth and social investment goals. Growth-enhancing spending is more short term, while well-being goals are typically achieved in the medium term, and are therefore not suited to satisfying the desires of impatient politicians (Ferrera, 2017). A continuous challenge for policymakers is to align the longer time horizons of social investment projects with standard planning and budgeting procedures in the member states. Projects typically run in the medium term (three–four years), and there are hitherto no structures in place that would help align time horizons in regional and social policymaking.

The fact that social and economic investments are typically discussed in different research and policy communities is a clear hindrance to the ability of the EU to promote inclusive growth (de la Porte, 2019). The Partnership Agreement (Chapter Two) linking projects more clearly to an overarching investment strategy in line with EU 2020 is a good start, as it promotes dialogue between regional, national and European actors; but we need more forceful efforts to promote learning about how to integrate social goals in regional development strategies, and we need rules that provide stronger incentives to integrate social goals, in order to avoid the existing adverse effects on income inequality in poor regions. Learning to exploit the strengths of both economic and social investments to the benefit of enhanced well-being will be an essential task.

Finally, there was no collective sense of urgency on social matters among governments in the EU in the observed period. In negotiations with the EU institutions, applying the economic and social ideas behind lifelong social investment has never been met with enthusiasm by the governments of EU member states (Ferrera, 2017). An exception is the emphasis on improving youth activity, which appears to be politically more expedient, in particular given that many EU member states have struggled to prevent the outflow of young people. Latvia, for example, struggles to provide bright prospects for its young people. The Latvian government adopted extensive measures to help those made most vulnerable by the crisis, such as the long-term unemployed, older workers in need of skills reorientation, disabled people who require supportive employment opportunities and marginalized communities where employment is scarce, but such measures could not prevent the emigration of 250,000 young people from Latvia during the crisis years.[2] Supporting young people is a cornerstone of EU regional policy. In Chapter Five, however, it was not possible to identify any EU social or economic investment effects on enhancing young people's prospects.

Absent clearer rules for budgeting and selecting projects that are useful to enhance *both* growth and regional well-being, we will continue to see weak or adverse well-being effects of EU spending.

Small amounts of social funding

The level of EU social investment continues to be too low. Chapter Two shows how social goals were mainstreamed into regional policy, particularly in the period 2000–06, which led to a more energized focus on intra-regional disparities, the urban–rural divide and concerns about poverty and social exclusion through directed, programmatic and regulatory mainstreaming. Nonetheless, social investments have largely remained constant at one fifth of the EU regional policy budget since 2000.

The crisis years 2007–12 saw several exceptional measures under EU regional policy. Greece was the target of several initiatives to facilitate Athens making better use of EU regional funding. Part of this package was an extra envelope of funding. but despite the obvious social effects of the crisis, it largely mirrored traditional regional funding priorities. Only €3.6 billion of the total €36 billion in structural and investment funds was made available from the ESF. Notable in this context was the €72 million from the Youth Employment Initiative, but this amount is tiny compared, for example, to the agricultural funding of almost €20 billion that was provided as part of the package.[3]

In the aftermath of the global financial crisis, societal challenges such as looming poverty and social exclusion attracted the attention of more and more European policymakers.[4] The Europe 2020 strategy set out in 2010 publicly confirmed Europe's commitment to the pursuit of social inclusion and the reduction of economic inequality and poverty among its citizens (European Commission, 2010a, 2010b). This led to the systematic addition of a number of social inclusion indicators to the EU's statistical database, which are referred to in the EU's regional policy regulatory framework (Eurostat, 2015). Despite this mainstreaming of social goals into the regulatory framework, however, the level of social investment remained low. Related, de la Porte and Natali (2018) have shown that the momentum of the social investment movement was lost during the crisis.

Thus, the 2014–20 framework continued in this direction. The ESF has been complemented by three additional funds. The Fund for European Aid to the Most Deprived (FEAD) helps some of the neediest through the provision of essential resources, such as basic necessities like food and clothing. The EU's Employment and Social Innovation (EaSI) programme offers assistance to those moving within Europe in search of better jobs and to social entrepreneurs in need of microfinancing. The European Globalization Adjustment Fund (EGF) assists redundant workers by giving them access to job training or financial assistance to set up their own businesses.[5] Nonetheless, EU social investments remain small compared to its economic investments (European Commission, 2014b).

Small amounts spread thinly and to richer areas

Relatively small amounts of funding are channelled into a large number of regions throughout the EU in pursuit of many objectives. Given the historically low levels of EU social spending, it is important to analyse whether these small amounts are concentrated in specific regions or spread more thinly. De Rynck and McAleavey noted in 2001 that: 'Priorities within Structural Fund programmes are sufficiently broad and flexible to satisfy diverse appetites during implementation' (De Rynck and McAleavey, 2001, p. 546). This observation still holds 20 years later. Putting small amounts of money into a large number of European regions is well known in European policy circles to be problematic.[6]

Figure 6.1 averages the social and economic investments in regions throughout the time period studied in this book, 1995–2013. The bulk of social investment is concentrated in Germany, Italy, Spain, the region around Warsaw and the north and west of the UK (Wales, Scotland and Northern Ireland). This illustrates that only a few regions have been able to attract large amounts of EU social investment, and that the lion's share of the social funds have been allocated in small chunks across regions. This funding pattern may also help to understand why Chapter Five found that the effects of EU social investment have been mixed at best.

Moreover, authorities at the regional level have incentives to choose experienced project partners because of the absorption pressures they are under, and because they want funding to flow to areas where corruption levels are low – especially in autonomous areas where such considerations are particularly important (Charron, 2016). Thus, EU funds typically benefit the richer municipalities (Dettmer and Sauer, 2018). The state of Rhineland-Palatinate in south-west Germany provides a useful example of this propensity. Rhineland-Palatinate, which historically relied heavily on the footwear industry, has over the past decades undergone a significant shift towards a service economy. EU regional spending has since the 1990s been used to diversify away from reliance on the manufacturing sector by developing active labour market policies, promoting technological development and converting military sites for industrial use.[7] In terms of the geographical concentration of EU spending within this region, EU funds mainly target the least deprived municipalities at the NUTS 3 level. The 10 most

Figure 6.1: EU regional funding across regions, 1995–2013

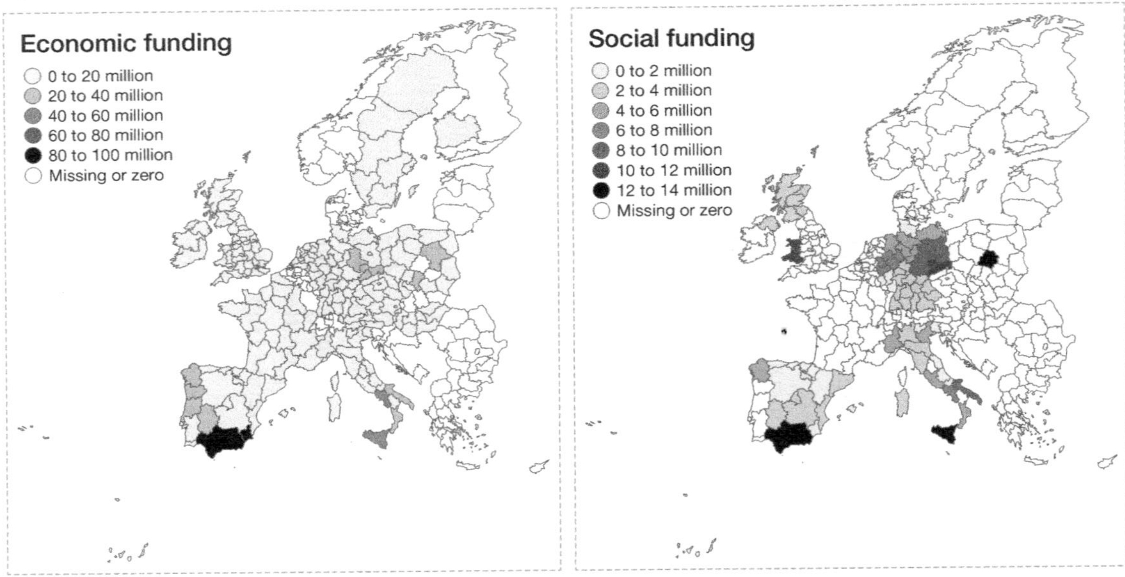

Notes: Inflation-adjusted payment data in millions of euros, averaged for the period 1995–2013. European Commission DG Regio Datawarehouse C3 and EU annual reports on structural funds. Left panel shows economic investments relative to regional GDP; right panel shows social investments relative to regional GDP. Social investment corresponds to ESF funding, whereas economic investment includes ERDF payments.

deprived areas in the state had a GDP in purchasing power standard (PPS) of between 51.3 per cent and 76.9 per cent of the EU-27 average but received less than 20 per cent of the EU funding. Conversely, the 10 richest areas had a GDP of between 109.8 per cent and 237 per cent of the EU-27 average but received about 35 per cent of the EU regional expenditure.[8]

Vote-seeking politics is not the source of the problem. The redistributive character of EU funds – which yield specific and visible benefits, while at the same time the costs are diffuse and obscure – means that domestic governments have incentives to claim credit for any positive spending effects that may arise. Thus, although political bias matters, most EU funding is spent on the basis of needs-related criteria (Bodenstein and Kemmerling, 2011; Chalmers, 2013; Schraff, 2014; Dellmuth et al, 2017) and an examination of whether political bias undermines EU funding effects found no evidence of this. Politically biased funding in the sense of the amount of funding distorted by vote-seeking politics does not systematically flow to regions where the funding was liable to yield the least benefit.[9] This conclusion is underlined by the standardized interviews, which suggest that the influence of partisan politics is limited, as only 29 per cent of the interviewed civil servants (*N*=32) thought that parliament at the national level was influential in the funds implementation process.

Informational asymmetries

Informational asymmetries about EU funding are harmful because project partners that benefit poor and otherwise vulnerable people may not be able to bid and receive any funding. There is a recurring pattern across various municipalities that information about EU funding availability, support networks and application processes tend not to be equally accessible to all potential beneficiaries. While it is the responsibility of the managing authority to provide potential beneficiaries with clear and detailed information on the conditions of eligibility, procedures and selection criteria for project funding, resource-poor municipalities still face dramatic informational asymmetries.[10]

Given this dynamic, project selection remains largely a top-down process in which local authorities and private sector organizations are less influential than regions, national authorities and the Commission. To help regions absorb earmarked funds, regional and national actors typically meet with a select number of potential partners that are already deemed eligible to receive EU funding at the beginning of a funding period. These meetings often include the same partners over time, especially in regions where public authorities' capacity is lower because less information flows to potentially eligible public and private actors, but also because regional networks are smaller and more exclusive.[11]

To illustrate this dynamic, the standardized interviews among civil servants in the EU dealing with regional policy implementation suggest that almost 80 per cent of the respondents considered management authorities at the national government level (*N*=130) and the Commission (*N*=129) to be influential in the funds implementation process, while only 43 per cent thought of local authorities as being influential (*N*=70). Moreover, when asked about the importance of specific tasks for the regional managing authorities, about 80 per cent of respondents thought it was somewhat or very important to coordinate with Commission officials (*N*=72), but only about 54 per cent of the respondents indicated it was somewhat or very important to coordinate with local authorities (*N*=72) and roughly 47 per cent thought it was somewhat or very important to gather information from interest groups, such as civil society organizations or business associations (*N*=63).

Indeed, 'traditional' regional policy directs top-down investment to poorer regions and there is no requirement to seek input from potential project partners (OECD, 2010). This, at least partially, explains why many private and public sector actors, even in highly developed regions, claim that they face severe informational gaps and asymmetries with regard to EU regional funding opportunities (Dellmuth, 2011b). Consider that only every other of the interviewed civil servants agreed somewhat or strongly with regard to the funds implementation process that 'the best advice on a proposed policy usually comes from the affected partners' (*N*=67).

As discussed in Chapter Two, the EU aims to promote a 'bottom-up' process in which local, regional and national public and private sector actors share information about needs and potential projects on the ground. This can then, in turn, be integrated into the regional funding strategy set out in the OPs for each region. But as regions need to be able to anticipate their absorption capacity about two years in advance, there is considerable pressure for projects to use their allocations early on in a multiannual budgetary framework. Since 2007, EU member states have been responsible for identifying a number of major projects that might be eligible for EU funding in order to ensure early absorption, and the N+3 (previously N+2) rule puts pressure on regional authorities to identify promising projects early on in a funding period.[12]

The incentives to select strong project partners early on, instead of soliciting contributions in an inclusive consultation process, mean that information about funding opportunities often fails to reach poorer municipalities and potential recipients that would be able to support socially weaker groups. Theoretically, workers, employers and civil society organizations should all be able to participate in the programming and management of the OPs. In practice, however, this seldom happens in a coordinated fashion. Especially in less affluent member states such as Portugal and Greece, OPs are identified in a top-down process during which potential final beneficiaries and the Commission are not sufficiently consulted.[13]

Even in the richer member states, such as Germany, there are regions in structural decline where inclusivity might be an issue. In Rhineland-Palatinate, a region introduced earlier, informational asymmetries that benefit rich areas (at NUTS level 3 and below) systematically prevent the inclusion of various municipalities in EU funding calls, possibly resulting in many good projects being overlooked.[14] In the region, many different public agencies are involved in the management of social investments channelled through the ESF alone.[15] This showcases that administrative complexity requires informal knowledge, short communication paths and good contacts for obtaining project funding – all of which are fostered by social capital. In addition, regional governments appear to have no systematic access to information about the final allocation of EU funds to final beneficiaries, a condition exemplified by the many questions asked by members of the German *Länder* parliaments about the distribution of EU regional funds.[16]

Thus, the EU funds implementation process is characterized by informational asymmetry that redounds to the benefit of those local groups that are resource-rich, well-organized and capable of mobilizing the resources, human as well as material, required to develop projects that are appealing from a funding standpoint.

Weak administrative capacity

In Chapter Three, I described challenges faced by regions with weak administrative or institutional capacity to manage funds. This aspect is inextricably linked to weak social capital, especially in poor regions. Social capital is known to foster interpersonal trust and inclusive networks, with beneficial effects on economic growth and inequality (Rothstein and Uslaner, 2005), as well as EU funding effects on economic growth (Cappelen et al, 2003; Becker et al, 2013). In the area of EU spending, shortfalls in social capital can imply that regional authorities are not able to collect all relevant information about EU fund allocations, identify partners and co-design funding applications.

Indeed, limited regional administrative capacity has been identified as a source of inefficiency or even mismanagement in EU funds implementation (Milio, 2007). Among the civil servants participating in the standardized interviews, 61 per cent somewhat or strongly agreed that 'some regions get more funding than others simply because they have more resources to improve the quality of their projects' (*N*=82).

Application processes are complex, and the applicants are dependent on the information provided by regional authorities. In poor regions in particular, networks between regional authorities, civil society and entrepreneurs are often weak. This means that it is often the small number of already strong actors capable of managing EU funds that apply for funding. Examples include local centres for medical doctors or law firms established with EU social funding.[17]

In poor regions, however, it is also often the case that lower-quality projects may be selected for funding or that projects may be badly implemented, as low levels of social capital can inhibit the capacity and network building that is essential for EU social investment projects to draw on. Sicily, which had a GDP per capita in Purchasing Power Parities (PPP) of about 60 per cent of the EU average in 2018, provides an extreme example. In July 2012, it became clear that there were irregularities in Sicily's management and audit system, and there was evidence of corruption and entanglement with the Mafia. As a result, the Commission suspended EU payments, and in July 2012 Sicily came under the direct control of Rome and a financial rescue plan was put in place.[18]

Regions, especially poor ones, often face the problem of there being too few project applications, or too many poor-quality applications that would not yield any measurable returns ('deadweight losses'). This is further exacerbated by information asymmetries about the existence of funding calls, how applications are supposed to be written and how grants should be managed.[19] In this context, regional entrepreneurs seeking funding for innovative projects are especially important to achieve an inclusive funding process that can also minimize uncertainty about absorption at the same time (cf Smyrl, 1997).

Due to shortfalls in capacity, regional and national governments frequently select the projects that appear convenient, for example by repurposing existing projects even if they only loosely fit EU funding goals. This is not penalized, as compliance audits to check the content of the project against a wider, coherent regional investment strategy are not carried out. Instead, 'performance audits' are conducted, where legality and regularity are centre stage, meaning whether regional funding of a project is in accordance with EU law. Attempts early in 2006 and in the period 2007–13 to push for compliance audits did not achieve consensus within the Court of Auditors – partly because of the perceived lack of capacity and partly because of the political sensitivity of the topic.[20] The Court of Auditors has in the past warned that EU legislation does not target funding directly at combating social issues such as child poverty, leading to insufficient funding efforts on the ground to tackle the issue,[21] but it does not have a systematic instrument to check regional and national actors' compliance with EU funding goals.

Taken together, given these structural barriers, it becomes clear that the regional and national authorities managing EU funding expect especially high and secure returns from project partners that are already experienced at handling public funds and are well capitalized. They are especially likely to choose such project implementers in poor regions. This helps to explain the absence of well-being effects and related capability effects in poor regions, as well as the adverse effects on distributive justice in poor regions discussed in Chapter Five. What is more, it is evident that those that want to promote EU social goals at the implementation stage will face an uphill battle. One such actor is the Commission, but the institution suffers from limitations in resources, such as the personnel required to do so systematically, and is under considerable pressure to spend the available budget.[22] While the Commission has generally established cooperation-oriented relations with actors at the regional and national levels (Bachtler and Mendez, 2007), there is evidence of pervasive conflicts and domestic actors' reluctance to devise projects in line with EU goals.[23] In line with this, my standardized interview material suggests that only 49 per cent of the interviewed civil servants thought that well-specified selection criteria were crucial for projects to be selected for funding (*N*=68). Only 35 per cent of the respondents somewhat or strongly agreed that 'top-level officials in the member states should carry out the Commission's decisions with absolute loyalty under all circumstances' (*N*=47).

Conclusion

This chapter has set out to provide an in-depth understanding of the findings in Chapter Five that EU social investments do not benefit poor and otherwise vulnerable people. Taken together, the document, news media and interview material analysed in this chapter points to five barriers to using EU social funds in ways that enhance well-being, which help to explain why EU social funds tend not to reach the poor and most disadvantaged people, but are instead mostly distributed among already wealthy actors in urban centres.

These dynamics are not inexorable, and existing calls for better integration of social goals into the EU's growth strategy have been made (Vandenbroucke et al, 2011; Hemerijck, 2013; Heins and de la Porte, 2014; Aranguiz, 2019). Moreover, economists and policymakers in the OECD and the EU social policy community have called for a rethink. That the unequal distribution of well-being that currently prevails is harmful to contemporary society and economic development is widely recognized, thanks largely to a group of economists and OECD policymakers that is pushing for a change in economic thinking to foster equitable growth (for example, Stiglitz et al, 2018; OECD, 2020a). EU regional funds are already providing social investments targeted at all stages of life. Changes in the regulatory framework and funding practices need to ensure that desirable effects can be enhanced and weak as well as adverse effects avoided.

In the ensuing Chapter Seven, I draw together the evidence from this book and contemplate the broader implications of the findings for inclusive growth and democratic legitimacy in the EU. In closing, I sketch avenues for future research.

SEVEN

Regional Well-Being, Inclusive Growth and EU Legitimacy

This concluding chapter provides a brief summary of the overall argument of the book, as well as an initial discussion of how it can be applied more broadly to improve inclusive growth and the EU's legitimacy in the eyes of citizens. The book closes by sketching areas for future research on the causes and consequences of well-being in the EU.

Summary of argument

This book argues that EU regional development should be conceptualized in terms of regional well-being, which emphasizes the distribution of wealth within regions. Regional well-being refers to a condition of distributive justice in a region, whereby poor and otherwise vulnerable people are provided with the capabilities needed to achieve the good quality of life they are striving for.

A firmer grasp of the ability of the EU to use its funds to improve regional well-being in its member states could help to remove the current barriers to achieving lasting well-being effects. Especially since the early 2000s, the EU's social goals have been increasingly mainstreamed into its legal framework governing regional development funding, and lifelong social investments in human capital have comprised about one fifth of the total structural and investment budget (Chapter Two). EU social investment co-finances domestic investment in education, healthcare and human capital, such as the renovation of university buildings and educational infrastructure, the provision of technical equipment, the building of medical centres and hospitals and support for vocational training projects or projects that integrate migrants into the labour market.

The ambition of this book is to better understand the effects of these EU social investments on regional well-being. The analysis has covered regional well-being in 16 of the 27 EU member states, with a combined population of 424 million in the period 1994–2013.[1]

In terms of *how* well-being has developed in the EU regions examined, the data clearly show that life is better in rich regions where labour markets tend to work better, young people have better prospects, public health is stronger and people are on average more highly skilled and have more social trust. That said, Europe has faced a poverty and economic inequality standstill in both rich and poor regions since the 1990s.

Moreover, the quantitative and qualitative evidence in this book suggests that EU funding in the studied regions has led to increased efforts to tackle socio-economic inequalities within regions, but currently still mostly benefits middle-income earners in rich regions. While this has led to positive EU spending effects on unemployment outcomes and participation in the labour force in rich regions, the evidence does not suggest any effects on health and youth inactivity. By contrast, I found adverse consequences for income inequality in poor regions. Economic investment does not appear to have any well-being effects.

These findings can be explained by a flawed regional policy framework and domestic funding practices that benefit the already wealthy. These practices might be in line with the EU's aim to strengthen the already existing human capital base to become a more competitive economy, but it has detrimental consequences for distributive justice, which backfire in the form of unfair growth and renewed Euroscepticism. Indeed, I find that regional and national authorities tend to select projects in ways that maximize their own interests,

and that there are powerful structural barriers to providing these authorities with incentives to pursue EU social goals forcefully: (a) social and economic investments remain largely siloed; (b) social funding amounts continue to be small; (c) small amounts are spread thinly and to richer areas; (d) informational asymmetries persist; and (e) shortfalls in administrative capacity in poor regions undermine the ability of resource-poor actors to attract EU funding.

Addressing these problems requires complementing the notion of *inter*-regional development that underpins Europe's growth policies and investments with a view of regional well-being as *intra*-regional well-being. It is my contention that the EU currently misses important opportunities to use regional investment policies to promote well-being within regions, which would be likely to have benefits for inclusive growth and citizens' belief in the legitimacy of the EU.

Implications for inclusive growth

The key aim of welfare state-related policies in all advanced democracies is to help solve the dilemma of how to achieve inclusive growth. Political scientists and economists have emphasized that there is a need to think about inclusive growth capable of counteracting the potentially negative implications of European integration for inequalities (Fitoussi et al, 2010; Stiglitz et al, 2018; Beckfield, 2019). In the EU, the ongoing debate about inclusive growth is focused on how to achieve a fair redistribution of wealth that benefits ordinary citizens (European Commission, 2014a, 2014b). However, a widespread belief in the EU in the utility of austerity measures has long curtailed public spending and led to market-oriented reforms, limiting the room for manoeuvre for those seeking to expand welfare states (Heins and de la Porte, 2014). But while European integration has exacerbated income inequality by encouraging austerity and welfare state retrenchment, 'retrenchment has not been "the only game in town". Rather, many countries have expanded new welfare policies such as "social investments"' (Busemeyer et al, 2018, p. 801).

The debate about social investment as an appropriate policy response lost momentum shortly after the financial crisis hit the European economy. By 2009, when the second Barroso Commission took office, the main issue on the EU agenda was stabilizing the eurozone area. It was widely believed that there was no room to expand EU social investments. Several political entrepreneurs continued to push for a stronger anti-poverty agenda even in times of crisis and, as a result, states and EU policymakers were persuaded that the EU needed to at least frame growth as more than a mere fiscal consolidation agenda that combined growth with social goals. One result was endorsement in 2010 of the aim to lift 20 million people out of poverty by 2020 and to reach an employment rate of 75 per cent by 2020 as key pillars of the Europe 2020 Strategy. Nonetheless, Europe has not seen any significant policy change to strengthen inclusive growth ever since the crisis (de la Porte and Natali, 2018).

That said, more recent events, such as the Annual Convention for Inclusive Growth in Brussels in May 2019, demonstrate that the conversation on the potential use of EU funding instruments to promote inclusive growth in a 'Social Europe' is ongoing.[2] This is perhaps unsurprising given that well-being-related challenges are having powerful political reverberations. The issue of inclusive growth is now widely debated as neither a distinctively socialist, social democratic, conservative nor new conservative programme, but about restoring a moral compass to existing growth policies. It is certainly the case that different political parties adopt specific electoral rhetoric and priorities with regard to the relationship between inequality and growth. As research on the 'social investment state' since the 2000s has shown, however, its legitimacy and effectiveness have been debated across political camps (Hemerijck, 2017). There are currently no significant political forces advocating a return to the passive and expansive welfare states of the post-war decades

(Piketty, 2014). Instead, a central question is how to use welfare state policies to invest in people throughout the course of their lives (Busemeyer et al, 2018).

As this book helps to explain, investing in human capital through the European Structural and Investment Funds benefits labour markets in rich regions, but reforms are necessary to help poor regions achieve similarly positive effects and to counteract negative effects of EU funding on income inequality. Partisan differences aside, acknowledging this in the public debate would be a first step towards overcoming the five existing barriers to the effective use of EU funding for well-being identified in Chapter Six.

Given these barriers, how could inclusive growth be strengthened? Social investments have consistently constituted about one fifth of the total EU regional policy budget since 2000, but the EU is not just a 'growth project' that helps to sustain poor jurisdictions or to shore up those experiencing economic stagnation (see also Barca, 2009; Bachtler et al, 2019). In reality, it is already promoting citizens' well-being in terms of enhanced labour market outcomes in rich regions, but these positive outcomes are mitigated by the fact that the funding effects are small and that adverse well-being effects are being recorded in poor regions. Future debate surrounding the reform of EU regional policy must explicitly acknowledge this reality.

However, in the EU there is a clear lack of political will to entrust the EU institutions with greater authority over social policy (Pierson, 1996). Absent leadership of powerful governments in the EU, funding is likely to continue to benefit already wealthy groups and the urban centres in regions. Poor areas in regions have been unable to capitalize on EU social investments as measured by well-being outcomes. Rich areas have greater capacity and more inclusive networks for attracting and using funds effectively, and therefore obtain greater returns to well-being. How regions can be supported to broaden their funding networks, make the funding process more bottom-up and support good projects in poor areas and projects that benefit poor people presents difficult challenges for the EU institutions and governments across the EU.

The Commission is already engaging in a wide range of activities expressed as 'soft power', such as communications, aides-memoire and white papers, that set out guidelines on funding at the outset of a funding period (Bachtler and Mendez, 2007). The Partnership Agreements under the most recent EU multiannual framework for 2014–20, in which regional and national actors must set out and justify their social investment strategy, are a step in the right direction, as they force domestic actors to think about the usefulness of projects for promoting well-being, including among the poorest and otherwise disadvantaged in society. However, the Commission faces capacity constraints at the outset of a multiannual financial framework that prevent it from efficiently monitoring the process in which regional and national authorities draw up their OPs and Partnership Agreements.

Increased accountability, for example through compliance audits with EU social goals, could provide incentives that kick-start such a dynamic. Regional policy has for the past 20 years been evaluated in terms of funding effects ('performance audits') rather than in terms of regional and national governments' compliance with EU goals when allocating EU funds across projects ('compliance audits'). The European Court of Auditors could use compliance audits to check the content of projects against a wider, coherent investment strategy. Such audits, supported by key member states, could be a first step towards holding domestic actors accountable for biasing funding towards wealthy groups and areas.

Simplifying funding rules would also facilitate the work towards using EU funding for well-being. Simplification can reduce the administrative burden and informational gaps in relation to EU funding (see also European Commission, 2011), and facilitate sharing information about EU funding and managing the funding received. This might be especially beneficial for the poorer regions that have capacity constraints. Further digitalization and simplification of eligibility rules would also be conducive to greater inclusivity. There is significant simplification potential in terms of the administrative burden associated with greater use of advanced electronic services for all information exchange between the administration and the beneficiaries. A move to better e-services could substantially reduce the burden of beneficiaries and make information more easily available to less resourceful areas that are currently missing out on many important funding possibilities.

Thus, the dynamics in EU regional funds allocation and practices are not immovable. In fact, my findings should hearten advocates of supranational fiscal redistribution, as a reformed EU regional policy can be a powerful instrument that can be deployed to improve well-being.

Implications for the EU's legitimacy in the eyes of citizens

Moreover, using EU spending to enhance regional well-being also promises to contribute to strengthening the EU's legitimacy. Regional disparities have undermined the EU's legitimacy in the eyes of citizens in the past (Lipps and Schraff, 2020). Legitimacy, the perception among citizens that the EU uses its authority appropriately, often measured using opinion polls on confidence or trust, is essential for the future viability of the EU (Dellmuth and Schlipphak, 2019). Legitimacy is a crucial resource for the EU to be able to pursue ambitious policies and garner state support. The more citizens, private and public sector organizations and domestic governments perceive the EU to be legitimate, the more readily the EU may be able to obtain resources, make decisions, secure compliance and, ultimately, solve problems (Tallberg et al, 2018).

EU regional funds have become tangible resources for many citizens. This provides both national governments and the EU with incentives to take credit for the funding. The FEB polls cited in Chapter One suggest that around 30–45 per cent of the citizens of all EU member states are aware of the EU support provided to their city or region. This is a considerable proportion that reflects a more general trend of growing public awareness of and debate about EU institutions and policies (Hooghe and Marks, 2009; De Wilde and Zürn, 2012), and the data suggest a consistent link between funding and awareness of the spending measures.

There is also an emerging debate about the effects of EU regional spending on public support for the EU, with some studies showing an effect of spending on EU support (Dellmuth and Chalmers, 2018; Schraff, 2019; but see López-Bazo and Royuela, 2019). People are known to evaluate the EU in terms of what it has done for them recently, and repeated positive experiences inform a more durable belief in the EU's legitimate right to make decisions that affect their lives (Scharpf, 2009).

What is more, research on the populist backlash has shown that it is easier for populist politicians to mobilize along income- and class-related cleavages when people feel economically insecure and left behind in an ever more globalized world. Thus, economic anxiety and distributional struggles are the base allowing populist politicians to mobilize support (Rodrik, 2018). In particular, Brexit has shown that economic divides across societal groups and across the urban–rural divide have contributed to an erosion of legitimacy vis-à-vis the EU (O'Reilly et al, 2016; Algan et al, 2017). In the poorest areas, many citizens might be expected eventually to turn against European integration and start supporting Eurosceptic political parties (Rodríguez-Pose, 2018; Dijkstra et al, 2019).

It will therefore be crucial to improve the effects of EU social investments on well-being in order to contribute to sustaining a base of popular support for the EU. Indeed, trust in the EU declined in most states following the global financial crisis of 2007–12, leading to the historically low levels of trust in 2013 (Foster and Frieden, 2017). However, as illustrated in Figure 7.1, trust has recovered since then in most of the EU member states examined (Denmark, France,

Figure 7.1: Percentage of citizens trusting the EU

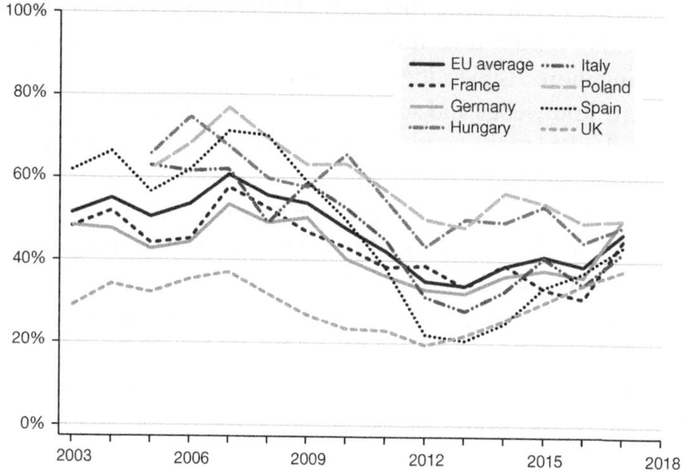

Note: Scale ranges from 'tend to trust' (1) to 'tend not to trust' (0). Number of respondents is c.1,000–2,000 per country covered. The EU average is based on data from the EU member states. Yearly measurement using poststratification weights.

Source: Standard Eurobarometer. See www.gesis.org/eurobarometer-data-service/search-data-access/data-access.

Germany, Italy and the UK), with the exception of Hungary and Poland, where EU trust has rather fluctuated since 2013. For example, in Poland, EU trust was still highest among the six states studied but has steadily declined from almost 80 per cent in 2007, following years of declining unemployment and increasing wealth after it joined the EU in 2004, to about 50 per cent in 2013, which is where it remained in 2017. The lowest levels of trust observed throughout the time period were found in the UK, where trust fluctuated between 20 and 40 per cent between 2003 and 2017, but where trust in the EU has increased by almost 20 percentage points since 2012.

EU officials are aware of this challenge. As far back as 2001, the Commission stated in its white paper on 'European governance' that the 'Union's credibility will eventually be judged by its ability to add value to national policies and address people's concerns more effectively at European and global level' (2001, p. 7). Structural funding is expressly cited as a tool for creating more visible added value for citizens that can improve citizens' knowledge and acceptance of EU policies, and in turn allow the EU to pursue more ambitious and effective policies to promote regional well-being.

It is crucial to advance the debate on how to reconcile the EU's regional and social policies with a more integrated approach to promoting growth and well-being, and thereby improve the EU's performance on well-being. There have been notable reforms of the European Employment Strategy and the ESF in recent years, and the European Pillar of Social Rights has also been established. These reforms showcase the broad consensus that the EU will need if it is to address social problems, but governments and EU policymakers remain too preoccupied with managing external shocks to the EU economy and ensuring growth, a trend that dovetails with the EU's ongoing investment strategies during the COVID-19 pandemic.

Avenues for future research

More extensive and sustained engagement with the insights derived from EU regional and social policy research, as well as interdisciplinary well-being research, would go a long way towards articulating a promising new research agenda on well-being in the EU. I outline three promising areas for future research.

The effects of EU spending on subjective well-being

Socio-economic relations are central to well-being, which makes 'objective well-being' an essential object of study.

Whether people are able to achieve a good quality of life is not just their responsibility alone, but instead depends on specific contextual factors that demonstrably facilitate the ability to obtain the good things in life. Early philosophical-theoretical work on welfare economics demonstrated that objective and subjective well-being are not necessarily connected (Sen, 1985). More recent research, however, suggests that there are contexts in which they may be strongly linked. That said, evidence of the effects of objective well-being on subjective well-being is typically limited to two indicators – income and income inequality (Katic and Ingram, 2017). In addition, previous research has concentrated on individual- and state-level indicators, and is therefore largely restricted to those levels of analysis in measuring any effects on either concept of well-being (Barrington-Leigh and Escande, 2018). Future research could usefully shed further light on the complex interlinkages between EU policies, regional well-being, and subjective well-being.

Public attitudes and EU spending effects

Previous scholarship has intimated that governments exploit public funds to buy votes. A core assumption is that this may have negative effects, but my research shows that vote-seeking politics is highly unlikely to undermine the effects of EU funding. How domestic redistributive and distributive politics in specific regions operate in conjunction with EU funding mechanisms to improve well-being, however, and the role of public attitudes toward the EU in this process, is still under-studied (see also Lipp and Schraff, 2019). This book provides a systematic, largely quantitative interrogation of EU funding effects on well-being, but there is much still to be learned about the causal mechanisms linking public opinion, including populist attitudes, and the politics of funding allocations with the well-being effects of EU spending. This could for example be achieved by conducting quantitative country case studies, which would make the examination of subnational EU spending, domestic politics, and public attitudes in their complexity more manageable.

EU spending effects on gender inequality

I have examined EU spending effects on indicators that capture the capabilities of people to access employment, education and healthcare and achieve a healthy and social life, aggregated at the regional level. I have also examined the effects on distributive justice, which foregrounds income inequality and poverty, taking account of income inequalities among the poor. However, a crucial policy development at supranational and global levels has been the promotion of income equality between men and women. Sex-based income differences are an integral part of the UN's Sustainable Development Goal 5 on gender equality, of the European Pillar of Social Rights and of the social policies and policy recommendations issued by many other global governance institutions. The OECD, for example, launched a 'Gender Initiative' in 2010 and has published several policy recommendations related to gender equality (OECD, 2011). The EU adopted a gender equality strategy for 2016–19 as a means of demonstrating its commitment to and promoting domestic gender equality legislation.

Nonetheless, gender equality measured in income differences is not typically included in well-being datasets (Barrington-Leigh and Escande, 2018), even though it is one of the measurements that captures non-economic well-being very well (McGillivray, 2005), and despite the fact that gender disparity-adjusted well-being indicators have been shown by a number of scholars to add useful insights (McGillivray and Pillarisetti, 2006). Although a few studies of subjective well-being focus on gender-related topics (for example, Uglanova, 2014), those focused on objective well-being do not ordinarily include gender equality measures.

If empirical investigations of well-being are to draw on normative conceptions of distributive justice, the question of whether measures of gender equality should be used as indicators of regional well-being must be confronted. Achieving gender equality is an important goal of various social policies. For example, welfare state policies that provide assistance with obtaining high-quality childcare and for the second career in a two-career household can help to reduce the penalties many women face in relation to career progression and working hours, as well as in wages, salaries and benefits (Esping-Andersen, 2007). The concept can therefore be considered an aspect of well-being and consonant with Sen's (1985) capabilities approach, but with a specific understanding of gender relations.

★★★

In closing, with its powerful insights into the sources of growth, regional policy analysis is central to our understanding of EU funding effects on cross-regional variations in GDP. However, future research needs to pay close attention to the distributional question. In this book, I seek to give the distribution of wealth among citizens within regions a greater place in the debate about EU spending. This debate requires more systematic and cumulative knowledge about existing inequalities and what the EU can do to remedy them.

The particular circumstances in 2021 are that there is a global health pandemic that has already cost the lives of almost a million people (Dong et al, 2020) and caused a global economic crisis. There are many possible future scenarios. One such scenario is that the current crisis will have similar effects to the 2007–12 crisis and further deepen socio-economic divisions in Europe. Another is that policymakers will use the pandemic as an opportunity to rethink regional development, finding responses that optimally balance efficiency and equity. One thing is clear from this book: EU regional funding needs to be reformed, given that over the past two decades it has had adverse effects on inequality in poor regions. The ongoing global economic crisis may provide the impetus needed to effectuate a paradigm shift within the EU towards embracing inclusive growth.

Appendix A: Qualitative and Standardized Interview Data

The interview evidence used in the book is derived from a series of semi-structured and standardized interviews. Between April 2008 and June 2010, I conducted 33 semi-structured interviews with EU policymakers, local and regional civil servants and employees of private organizations. The interviewees were asked a range of questions regarding the professional mission statement they were expected to uphold, their institutional position, their interactions with others when implementing EU regional funds and the challenges and opportunities they associate with EU funding.

Additional standardized interviews were conducted among civil servants involved in EU funds implementation between June and November 2012. Prospective participants were contacted first by letter or telephone, and then by an email which contained a link to an online questionnaire. Given the likelihood that experiences with EU funding are not uniform among member states, respondents were recruited to represent a variety of states in different EU geographical areas. In total, 156 officials participated from 19 EU member states (see Tables A.1 and A.2). Since the interviews were intended to yield expert opinions on EU spending, the survey is based on a sample of respondents who were each identified as the most knowledgeable person in the relevant ministry on EU regional policy. The questionnaire consisted of 18 questions. It was developed in English and was translated into German, French, Polish and Portuguese (available upon request). For the entire questionnaire, see the online supplementary information available for this book.

Table A.1: Number of respondents per country

Country	Number of observations
Austria	18
Belgium	4
Denmark	2
Germany	44
Greece	1
Finland	5
France	16
Ireland	7
Italy	6
Luxemburg	2
Netherlands	2
Portugal	11
Spain	20
Sweden	6
UK	12
Total	156

Table A.2: Number of respondents per work category

Work category	Number of observations
In public administration on federal level	34
In the regional public administration	117
In the local public administration	5
Total	156

Appendix B: EU Social and Economic Investments*

Description of social funding targets

Health: Air quality; environmental and health infrastructure; integrated prevention and pollution control; management and distribution of drinking and waste water; noise; public health; promotion of clean urban transport.

Human capital: Actions by professionals (including vocational training); advanced support services for firms and groups of firms; agriculture-specific vocational training; assistance to research and technology development (R&TD), particularly in small and medium-sized enterprises (SMEs), including access to R&TD services in research centres; assistance to SMEs with the promotion of environmentally friendly products and production processes; assisting large business organizations; design and dissemination of innovative and more productive ways of organizing work; design, introduction and implementation of educational reforms; developing educational and vocational training (for persons or firms); developing human potential in research and innovation, in particular through postgraduate studies, the training of researchers and networking activities connecting universities, research centres and businesses; development of lifelong learning systems and strategies within firms; development of specific services for employment, training and support for restructuring sectors and firms, and developing systems to anticipate economic change and future workplace requirements in terms of jobs and skills; educational infrastructure; forestry-specific vocational training;

* The data from Appendix B are from DG Region Datawarehouse C3 and the various annual reports of the Structural Funds.

implementing active and preventive measures in the labour market; innovation and technology transfers, establishment of networks and partnerships between business and/or research institutes; integrated projects for urban and rural regeneration; investment in firms directly linked to research and innovation; LEADER+; measures for improving access to and efficient use of information and communication technologies (ICTs) by SMEs; modernization and strengthening of labour market institutions; other measures to stimulate research, innovation and entrepreneurship in SMEs; pathways to integration and re-entry into employment for women and disadvantaged groups; research projects based in universities and research institutes; research, technological development and innovation (RTDI); support for young farmers; support for self-employment and business start-ups; training for researchers.

Social inclusion: Childcare and housing infrastructure; integrated projects for urban and rural regeneration; measures to encourage active ageing and prolong working lives; pathways to integration and employment re-entry for women and disadvantaged groups; social inclusion.

Description of economic funding targets

Agriculture: Adjustment of fishing effort, defined as fleet capacity (tonnage and engine power) multiplied by days at sea; agricultural water resources management; aquaculture; development and improvement of infrastructure connected with the development of agriculture; development of cultural infrastructure; diversification of agricultural activities; encouragement of craft activities; encouragement of tourism-related activities; equipment for fishing ports and coastal protection; establishment of associations of forest holders; fisheries; forestry; improving and maintaining the ecological stability of protected woodlands; improving the harvesting, processing and marketing of forestry; improving the processing and marketing of agricultural products; land improvement; marketing of quality agricultural products; meeting standards; use of farm advisory services; rehabilitation of industrial sites and contaminated land; non-physical investments (development and provision of tourism-related services, sporting, cultural and leisure activities, heritage); physical investment (information centres, tourist accommodation, catering facilities); planting of non-farm land; processing, marketing and promotion of fisheries products; protection and development of natural heritage; promoting new outlets for the use and marketing of forestry products; promoting the adaptation and development of rural areas; protection and preservation of the cultural heritage; renewal and modernization of the fishing fleet; setting up of farm relief and farm management services; support for young farmers.

Infrastructure: Airports; basic services for the rural economy and population; cycle tracks; ICTs; inland waterways (regional and local); intelligent transport systems; investment in physical capital (plant and equipment); mobile rail assets; motorways; multimodal transport; national roads; ports; railways; regional/local roads; renovation and development of villages, and protection and conservation of the rural heritage; technology transfer and improvement of cooperation networks; telecommunications infrastructure and information society; telephone infrastructure (including broadband networks); urban transport.

Energy: Collection, storage, treatment and distribution of drinking water; Environmentally friendly, clean and economical energy technologies; energy efficiency, co-generation, energy management; electricity, gas, petrol and solid fuel energy infrastructures; natural gas; petroleum products; upgrading and rehabilitation of industrial and military sites; renewable energy: biomass, solar, wind power, solar power, hydro-electricity, biomass, geothermal and other.

Appendix C: Measuring Poverty and Inequality

Net equivalized household income

Using the ECHP and EU-SILC household survey data introduced in Chapter Four, I followed Eurostat standard practice and weighted household members by using the Eurostat and OECD equivalence scale. The scale assigns a weight to each household member and then adds the resulting figures to arrive at the equivalized household size: 1.0 to the first adult; 0.5 to the second adult and each subsequent person aged 14 and over; and 0.3 to each child under the age of 14 (see also Castells-Quintana et al, 2015).

Weights

Equivalized data on household income were used to calculate poverty and income inequality using cross-sectional household weights. The 'design weights' at the level of households were calculated by taking the inverse of each of the household inclusion probabilities (cf European Commission, 2010c). To aggregate this measure at the regional level, I used household weights and adjusted for price changes over time (cf Mack and Lange, 2015).

Poverty line

When running analyses at the NUTS level, the use of regional-level poverty lines would provide a relative measure of poverty determined only by intra-regional income distribution, wholly independent of any regional disparities that might exist in the country. By contrast, using national-level poverty lines, which the EU typically defines as below 60 per cent of the national median income and uses to calculate such measures as risk of poverty (European Commission, 2010c, p. 12), would introduce an element of 'absoluteness' to the data, as the resulting poverty rate in a NUTS region would then depend on differences in income levels among NUTS regions either within the same country or within the EU. The 'higher' the geographical level at which the poverty line is expressed, the more relative the poverty measure becomes (cf Verma et al, 2006). To introduce elements of difference both within and across EU regions, I demarcated poverty lines at 60 per cent of the national median income, calculated separately for each state and year to factor in overall increases in living standards (cf Atkinson et al, 2002, p. 79).

Creating poverty measures

The general formula for the Foster-Greer-Thorbecke (FGT) index is as follows:

$$P_{\alpha} = \frac{1}{N}\sum_{i=1}^{N}\left(\frac{G_i}{z}\right)^{\alpha}, \quad (\alpha \geq 0) \qquad (1)$$

where α reflects the sensitivity of the index to poverty gaps. The larger *a* is, the greater the measure's sensitivity to poverty gaps. The poverty line is z, and the value of disposable household income for the i-th household is x_i. The poverty gap for individual i is G_i=z-x_i.

Creating income inequality measures

The Gini coefficient is based on the Lorenz curve, a cumulative frequency measure that compares the distribution of income with a uniform distribution that represents equality. The formula is as follows:

$$Gini = 1 - \frac{1}{N}\sum_{i=1}^{N}(x_i - x_{i-1})(y_i + y_{i-1}) \qquad (2)$$

where x_i is a point on the X-axis, and y_i a point on the Y-axis.

The formula for measuring generalized entropy (GE) takes the following general form:

$$GE(\alpha) = \frac{1}{\alpha(\alpha - 1)}\left[\frac{1}{N}\sum_{i=1}^{N}\left(\frac{y_i}{\bar{y}}\right)^{\alpha} - 1\right] \qquad (3)$$

where $\bar{y}$ is the mean income in region i (see also World Bank Institute, 2014). The lower α is, the more the measure is sensitive to changes at the bottom part of the distribution; for higher values, it is more sensitive to changes at the top (Atkinson and Bourguignon, 2015).

Appendix D: Patterns of Regional Well-Being

Table D.1: Well-being indicators and their correlates, by funding period and type of region

	1994–99		2000–06		2007–13	
	Richer regions	**Poorer regions**	**Richer regions**	**Poorer regions**	**Richer regions**	**Poorer regions**
Capabilities						
Unemployment	9.24%*	14.57%*	6.93%*	12.52%*	8.43%*	12.71%*
Employment	41.50%*[a]	36.36%*[a]	43.04%*	38.21%*	43.81%*	38.52%*
Inactive youth	Missing	Missing	10.00%*	15.46%*	11.34%*	14.28%*
Infant mortality	4.69*	6.22*	3.97*	4.44*	3.22*	4.20*
Self-perceived health	60.64%*	57.64%*	64.22%*	60.95%*	70.66%*	67.24%*
Distributive justice[b]						
FGT (α=0): Head count ratio	22.56%*	14.54%*	21.91%*	12.43%*	18.47%*	14.50%*
FGT (α=1): Poverty gap index	0.08*	0.05*	0.07*	0.03*	0.06*	0.04*
FGT (α=2): Squared poverty gap index	0.05*	0.03*	0.04*	0.02*	0.04*	0.03*
Gini coefficient	0.30*	0.27*	0.29*	0.26*	0.28	0.28
GE (α=1): Theil index	0.16*	0.13*	0.15*	0.13*	0.16	0.17

	1994–99		2000–06		2007–13	
GE (α=2): Squared coeff. of variation	0.19	0.19	0.17	0.17	0.19	0.25
P90/10	4.16	4.09	4.10*	3.67*	4.13	3.99
P90/50	1.89	1.94	1.94	1.89	1.99	1.97
GDP per capita, PPP (as % EU average)	106.85%*	65.88%*	113.84%*	84.83%*	110.15%*	66.55%*

Notes: Figures are regional averages. Asterisks denote statistical significance ($p<0.05$) from two-tailed t-tests assuming unequal variances, which test whether mean differences differ between poor and rich regions in each MFF. [a] Values for 1999. [b] Distributive justice indicators are not available for 2013 as the number of observations in the highest and lowest income categories of the EU-SILC was too low; the averages in the final two columns are for the period 2007–12.

Table D.2: Change in regional well-being indicators and GDP

	1994–99		2000–06		2007–13	
	Richer regions	**Poorer regions**	**Richer regions**	**Poorer regions**	**Richer regions**	**Poorer regions**
Capabilities						
Unemployment	-24.56	-2.31	-6.68	-12.89	54.68	51.13
Employment	Missing	Missing	4.39	7.17	-5.13	-5.93
Inactive youth	Missing	Missing	-3.61	-11.51	23.60	24.00
Infant mortality	-27.98	-26.77	-17.73	-27.10	-13.07	-13.66
Self-perceived health	-11.71	-8.16	16.16	20.05	-2.24	-0.93
Distributive justice[a]						
FGT (α=0): Head count ratio	-21.03	-14.65	-9.28	-8.99	-22.38	-0.09
FGT (α=1): Poverty gap index	-36.07	-21.35	-16.49	-14.46	-31.48	12.73
FGT (α=2): Squared poverty gap index	-47.35	-21.30	18.72	-15.19	-41.58	13.70
Gini	-11.08	-14.46	3.87	-0.52	-7.4	2.4
GE (α=1): Theil index	-24.01	-27.69	-0.02	-1.34	64.30	70.94

	1994–99		2000–06		2007–13	
GE (α=2): Squared coeff. of variation	-27.44	-35.57	-1.34	-11.49	68.61	59.57
P90/10	-11.70	-15.80	25.07	2.04	-20.57	-6.03
P90/50	-3.90	-8.14	8.92	1.66	-7.24	1.64
GDP per capita, PPP (as % EU average)	7.02	4.93	-1.88	4.88	0.90	3.46

Notes*:* Percentage change and percentage point change are calculated for the averages of the indicators shown in Table E.1. [a] Distributive justice indicators are not available for 2013; the changes in the final two columns are for the period 2007–12.

Table D.3: Gini standard deviation, average and change

	Average SD	**Difference in averages**	**Difference in averages**
	2004–12	**2004–12**	**2008–12**
Czech Republic	3.480	-0.677	-1.923
Spain	3.999	0.532	-1.192
Finland	1.862	0.246	-1.655
France	4.355	-0.170	-0.184
UK	3.463	–	-0.425

Notes: SD=Standard deviation. The difference in the averages is calculated as the SD for a country at the end of an observed time period minus the SD for the same country at the beginning of an observed time period.

Table D.4: London-excluded Gini standard deviation, average and change

	Average SD	**Difference in averages**	**Difference in averages**
	2004–11	**2004–11**	**2008–11**
Czech Republic	3.480	-0.473	-1.923
Spain	3.999	0.236	-1.192
Finland	1.862	-0.783	-1.655
France	4.355	1.156	-0.184
UK	2.681	-4.448	-2.359

Notes: SD=Standard deviation. Given that London is an extreme outlier in the sense that it suffers from much higher income inequality than other capital cities in Europe (Chapter Four), I provide these figures excluding London. The difference in averages is calculated as the SD for a country at the end of an observed time period minus the SD for the same country at the beginning of an observed time period.

Appendix E: Determinants of Regional Well-Being

In Chapter Five, I use fixed effects regression with well-being measurements as the dependent variables. The choice of fixed effects regressions is supported by Hausman tests (p-value<0.000 for all indicators). The different measures yield no evidence for unit roots, as augmented Dickey-Fuller tests with one lag rejected the null hypothesis that all panels contain unit roots for all well-being indicators (p-value<0.001 for all indicators). Models are thus estimated in levels. Following Lagrange multiplier tests, annual dummies are included (p<0.000 for all well-being indicators) in all models. This holds potentially unobserved time-specific variables, such as crisis years that could affect well-being outcomes, constant.

Consistent with prior practice, models are indexed by time t and NUTS regions i (see equation 1):

$$y_{it} = \beta \mathbf{X}_{it} + \alpha_i + \delta_t + u_{it} \tag{4}$$

where y is the well-being achievement, $\boldsymbol{X}$ is a vector of independent variables, α_i is a fixed effect component included to capture unobserved heterogeneity among EU regions, and δ_t is an annual fixed effect introduced to control for unobserved factors common to all regions.

Several dependent variables (employment, Theil index, squared coefficient of variation, and P90/10) were logarithmized to avoid biased estimates, given that they are highly skewed. Logarithmization was taken into account when calculating effect size.

A series of Arellano-Bond tests indicated the presence of first-order autocorrelation for the various well-being indicators. Thus, I reported Driscoll-Kraay standard errors that are robust to general forms of spatial and temporal dependence and clustered them at the level of regions.

Table E.1: Panel regression of capability indicators on EU social investments, all regions

	(1)	(2)	(3)	(4)	(5)
	Unemployment	**Employment (log)**	**Youth inactivity**	**Infant mortality**	**Self-perceived health**
EU social investments (log) (*t-1*)	-0.488*** (0.126)	0.003 (0.002)	-0.237* (0.108)	-0.049 (0.073)	0.002 (0.004)
EU social investments (log) (*t-2*)	-0.546*** (0.150)	0.007*** (0.002)	-0.401*** (0.077)	0.006 (0.058)	0.008* (0.004)
Union density (*t-1*)	0.059 (0.151)	-0.001 (0.002)	0.231 (0.164)		
Population density (log)	5.161 (4.562)	-0.034 (0.035)	2.888 (2.435)	6.724*** (1.892)	0.025*** (0.008)
GDP growth (*t-1*)	-25.222*** (4.913)	0.239*** (0.070)	-13.044*** (3.932)	2.648* (1.457)	0.036 (0.126)
National health spending (*t-1*)				-0.121* (0.068)	0.033*** (0.007)
Number of observations	1,746	1,793	1,566	1,799	669
Number of regions	153	154	151	142	86
R^2 (within)	0.223	0.275	0.198	0.430	0.448

Notes: Figures are unstandardized coefficients from two-way fixed effects panel regression models, with annual fixed effects included in each model and Driscoll-Kraay standard errors in parentheses. A constant term is included in each regression but not reported for the sake of brevity. Significance levels: * $p<0.10$, ** $p<0.05$, *** $p<0.01$.

Table E.2: Panel regression of capability indicators on EU social investments, rich regions

	(1)	(2)	(3)	(4)	(5)
	Unemployment	**Employment (log)**	**Youth inactivity**	**Infant mortality**	**Self-perceived health**
EU social investments (log) (*t-1*)	-0.200 (0.162)	0.003 (0.003)	-0.055 (0.109)	-0.003 (0.090)	0.006 (0.005)
EU social investments (log) (*t-2*)	-0.546*** (0.096)	0.008*** (0.001)	-0.640*** (0.144)	0.023 (0.075)	0.004 (0.003)
Union density (*t-1*)	0.136 (0.142)	-0.002 (0.002)	0.352*** (0.099)		
Population density (log)	1.207 (1.316)	-0.016 (0.015)	0.891 (0.840)	2.374* (1.193)	0.018** (0.007)
GDP growth (*t-1*)	-8.424** (3.398)	0.099* (0.055)	-8.412** (3.161)	-1.059 (0.904)	0.092 (0.089)
National health spending (*t-1*)				-0.332*** (0.095)	0.028*** (0.007)
Number of observations	1,070	1,093	947	1,067	448
Number of regions	102	103	99	90	58
R^2 (within)	0.317	0.351	0.337	0.356	0.517

Notes: Figures are unstandardized coefficients from two-way fixed effects panel regression models, with annual fixed effects included in each model and Driscoll-Kraay standard errors in parentheses. A constant term is included in each regression. Significance levels: * p<0.10, ** *0*<0.05, *** p<0.01.

Table E.3: Panel regression of capability indicators on EU social investments, poor regions

	(1)	(2)	(3)	(4)	(5)
	Unemployment	**Employment (log)**	**Youth inactivity**	**Infant mortality**	**Self-perceived health**
EU social investments (log) (*t-1*)	-0.514** (0.173)	0.006 (0.004)	0.108 (0.087)	-0.129 (0.077)	-0.018 (0.011)
EU social investments (log) (*t-2*)	-0.259 (0.158)	0.003 (0.003)	-0.034 (0.132)	-0.012 (0.039)	0.037** (0.015)
Union density (*t-1*)	0.426 (0.295)	-0.011*** (0.003)	0.043 (0.216)		
Population density (log)	38.655** (17.128)	-0.066 (0.211)	14.712** (6.079)	-0.227 (2.583)	0.355 (0.241)
GDP growth (*t-1*)	-12.772 (8.749)	0.154* (0.077)	-1.504 (6.278)	0.846 (2.438)	0.065 (0.174)
National health spending (*t-1*)				-0.052 (0.199)	0.042 (0.034)
Number of observations	493	517	468	536	202
Number of regions	71	71	66	65	34
R^2 (within)	0.343	0.307	0.212	0.458	0.429

Notes: Figures are unstandardized coefficients from two-way fixed effects panel regression models, with annual fixed effects included in each model and Driscoll-Kraay standard errors in parentheses. A constant term is included in each regression. Significance levels: * $p<0.10$, ** $p<0.05$, *** $p<0.01$.

Table E.4: Panel regression of distributive justice indicators on EU social investments, all regions

	(1)	(2)	(3)	(4)	(5)
	Squared poverty gap index	**Gini coefficient**	**Theil index (log)**	**Squared coefficient of variation (log)**	**P90/10 (log)**
EU social investments (log) (*t-1*)	0.002 (0.001)	0.147 (0.228)	0.019 (0.028)	0.026 (0.045)	-0.004 (0.015)
EU social investments (log) (*t-2*)	-0.001 (0.002)	-0.283 (0.289)	-0.046 (0.035)	-0.081 (0.064)	0.028* (0.013)
Population density (log)	0.030 (0.112)	0.853 (9.336)	-0.490 (0.713)	-1.315 (1.092)	0.804* (0.436)
GDP growth (*t-1*)	0.023 (0.029)	3.423 (8.485)	0.384 (0.751)	0.619 (1.104)	0.037 (0.312)
Tertiary education	0.037** (0.016)	-1.601 (1.880)	-0.040 (0.153)	0.140 (0.232)	-0.144 (0.116)
National educational spending (*t-1*)	0.004 (0.003)	-1.288*** (0.245)	-0.086*** (0.026)	-0.081 (0.046)	-0.066*** (0.018)

	(1)	(2)	(3)	(4)	(5)
	Squared poverty gap index	**Gini coefficient**	**Theil index (log)**	**Squared coefficient of variation (log)**	**P90/10 (log)**
Number of observations	543	544	544	544	542
Number of regions	85	85	85	85	85
R^2 (within)	0.076	0.079	0.076	0.061	0.104

Notes: Figures are unstandardized coefficients from two-way fixed effects panel regression models, with annual fixed effects included in each model and Driscoll-Kraay standard errors in parentheses. A constant term is included in each regression. Significance levels: * $p<0.10$, ** $p<0.05$, *** $p<0.01$.

Table E.5: Panel regression of distributive justice indicators on EU social investments, rich regions

	(1)	(2)	(3)	(4)	(5)
	Squared poverty gap index	**Gini coefficient**	**Theil index (log)**	**Squared coefficient of variation (log)**	**P90/10 (log)**
EU social investments (log) (*t-1*)	0.000 (0.001)	0.530 (0.515)	0.071 (0.061)	0.125 (0.093)	-0.000 (0.017)
EU social investments (log) (*t-2*)	0.003* (0.001)	-0.263 (0.450)	-0.031 (0.049)	-0.040 (0.086)	0.006 (0.009)
Population density (log)	0.094 (0.098)	-6.550 (5.175)	-1.482*** (0.464)	-2.945*** (0.883)	0.490 (0.303)
GDP growth (*t-1*)	-0.015 (0.024)	-6.482 (9.119)	-0.149 (0.843)	0.244 (1.369)	-0.362 (0.420)
Tertiary education	0.011 (0.020)	-8.010* (4.081)	-0.607 (0.348)	-0.721 (0.524)	-0.410 (0.265)
National educational spending (*t-1*)	0.004 (0.003)	-1.623*** (0.489)	-0.106** (0.048)	-0.091 (0.081)	-0.087*** (0.020)
Number of observations	362	364	364	364	364
Number of regions	57	57	57	57	57
R^2 (within)	0.107	0.129	0.120	0.100	0.125

Notes: Figures are unstandardized coefficients from two-way fixed effects panel regression models, with annual fixed effects included in each model and Driscoll-Kraay standard errors in parentheses. A constant term is included in each regression. Significance levels: * $p<0.10$, ** $p<0.05$, *** $p<0.01$.

Table E.6: Panel distributive justice indicators on EU social investments, poor regions

	(1)	(2)	(3)	(4)	(5)
	Squared poverty gap index	**Gini coefficient**	**Theil index (log)**	**Squared coefficient of variation (log)**	**P90/10 (log)**
EU social investments (log) (*t-1*)	0.042** (0.016)	5.574** (1.863)	0.380** (0.134)	0.527** (0.236)	0.052 (0.113)
EU social investments (log) (*t-2*)	0.003 (0.007)	2.462** (1.002)	0.185* (0.085)	0.203 (0.132)	0.033 (0.074)
Population density (log)	0.036 (0.186)	3.284 (18.577)	-0.055 (1.229)	-0.795 (1.656)	0.735 (1.044)
GDP growth (*t-1*)	-0.021 (0.031)	-6.732 (4.299)	-0.733* (0.387)	-1.259* (0.603)	-0.486 (0.478)
Tertiary education	0.088 (0.057)	12.735 (7.961)	0.941* (0.447)	1.515* (0.703)	0.674 (0.820)
National educational spending (*t-1*)	-0.002 (0.008)	-1.029 (1.385)	0.015 (0.094)	0.070 (0.123)	-0.070 (0.080)
Number of observations	169	168	168	168	166
Number of regions	34.	34	34	34	34
R^2 (within)	0.161	0.157	0.176	0.246	0.127

Notes: Figures are unstandardized coefficients from two-way fixed effects panel regression models, with annual fixed effects included in each model and Driscoll-Kraay standard errors in parentheses. A constant term is included in each regression. Significance levels: * p<00.10, ** p<0.05, *** p<0.01.

Notes

Chapter One

1 Although the crisis is often referred to in the literature as the '2008 crisis', following the sub-prime crash in 2008, I locate the crisis between 2007 and 2012 (see also Tooze, 2018), which is when world GDP growth was negative. World GDP growth became positive again in 2013 (World Development Indicators, 2020).

2 Regions are classified on the basis of existing political and administrative regional tiers, where pre-existing structures are lacking, on the basis of population. The average size of NUTS regions is within the following population thresholds: 3–7 million for NUTS 1 regions, 800,000–3 million for NUTS 2 regions and 150,000–800,000 for NUTS 3 regions. The most recent amendment to the original 2003 regulation establishing the NUTS regions is Commission Delegated Regulation 2019/1755 of 8 August 2019.

3 These are figures for earmarked regional funding during the period 2014–20.

4 Funding through the Cohesion Fund and smaller funding programs such as the so-called 'Community initiatives' during 2000–06 cannot be broken down by region and is therefore not included in the analysis.

5 The figures for 2014–20 are estimates of earmarked (or 'committed') funding, see European Commission (2011).

Chapter Two

1 For the purposes of this study, it makes sense to examine stage three (project generation) and four (project management), suggested by Tödtling-Schönhofer et al (2014) as one stage, as I do not provide a performance evaluation of specific bureaucratic procedures.

2 Interviews, top-level civil servant, DG Regio, 4 February 2010; head of unit, DG Regio, 24 February 2010.

3 Interview, head of unit, European Court of Auditors, 16 February 2010.

4 Interview, top-level civil servant, DG Regio, 4 February 2010.

5 Interview, head of department, Chamber of Commerce Rhein-Neckar, Germany, 5 March 2010.

6 Interview, director, City Hall Mannheim, 6 June 2010.

7 These categories are inspired by Wamsler's (2015) analysis of environmental policy mainstreaming.

8 27–28 June 1988, Hanover (Hannover Messe), chaired by Helmut Kohl. 11–12 February 1988, Brussels (Charlemagne Building), chaired by Helmut Kohl. www.consilium.europa.eu/en/european-council/conclusions/1992-1975/.

9 Press releases of the European Commission from April 1992, available at http://europa.eu/rapid/press-release_IP-91-368_en.htm, and from May 1992, available at http://europa.eu/rapid/press-release_MEMO-92-5_en.htm.

10 Council Regulation (EEC) No 2052/88 of 24 June 1988 on the tasks of the Structural Funds and their effectiveness and on coordination of their activities between themselves and with the operations of the European Investment Bank and the other existing financial instruments; Council Regulation (EC) No 1260/1999 of 21 June 1999 laying down general provisions on the Structural Funds; Council Regulation (EC) No 1083/2006 of 11 July 2006 laying down general provisions on the European Regional Development Fund, the European Social Fund and the Cohesion Fund and repealing Regulation (EC) No 1260/1999.

11 Interviews, head of unit, Committee of the Regions, 2 February 2010; MEP and former top-level civil servant in DG Regio, 24 February 2010.

12 Euractiv press release, 'Socialists, centre-right quibble over eurozone reforms', 17 March 2011; Euractiv press release, '"Calculating real recovery" what is fair growth in Europe?', 26 May 2011; Euractiv press release, 'PES Fair Growth Conference: "Transparency is a weapon of mass destruction of privileges" says EU Commissioner Pierre Moscovici', 26 March 2015.

13 For example, Europe Daily Bulletin, 'Commission wants to mobilise EFSM for €7 billion', Brussels: Agence Europe, 16 July 2015; Europe Daily Bulletin, 'Towards budget neutrality of national contributions to EFSI', Brussels: Agence Europe, 12 January 2015.

14 This is the case for both EU social funding per capita and inflation-adjusted EU social funding per capita.

15 Interview, head of unit, DG Regio, 24 February 2010.

16 Interviews, top-level civil servant, DG Regio, 4 February 2010; MEP and former top-level civil servant in DG Regio, Brussels, 24 February 2010.

17 Interviews, top-level civil servant, Federal Ministry for Economic Affairs and Energy, 6 June 2009; former top-level civil servant, regional government of Bavaria, Germany, 17 March 2010.

18 Interviews, head of unit, Committee of the Regions, 2 February 2010; MEP, Progressive Alliance, 3 February 2010; MEP, Greens, 28 January 2010; Christian Democrats, 28 January 2010.

19 Interview, senior civil servant, DG Regio, 2 October 2010.

20 Interviews, head of unit, European Court of Auditors, 16 February 2010; top-level civil servant, DG Regio, 4 February 2010.

21 Interview, head of unit, European Court of Auditors, 16 February 2010.

22 Interviews, MEP and former top-level civil servant in DG Regio, Brussels, 24 February 2010; top-level civil servant, DG Regio, 4 February 2010.

23 Interviews, head of unit, European Court of Auditors, 16 February 2010; top-level civil servant, DG Regio, 4 February 2010.

Chapter Three

1 Note that this interpretation of the location of justice is somewhat controversial among political philosophers (see, e.g., Young, 2011).

2 Given the geographically aggregated nature of the EU spending data, it has not been possible to study such effects directly (see also Mohl and Hagen, 2011), but the results of the regression analyses in Chapter Five on the effects of EU funding on regional well-being can be interpreted with reference to Matthew effects.

3 These results are underscored by two-sample t-tests that assume equal variances ($p<0.000$ for highly skilled workers, $N=2{,}216$; $p<0.000$ for social trust; $N=1{,}219$).

4 This finding is supported by a two-sample t-test with equal variances using the author's *Regional Well-Being Dataset* introduced in Chapter Four ($N=2410$; $p=0.000$).

Chapter Four

1 Since this is a regional-level analysis, smaller states that are not divided into regions for the purpose of EU funding, such as Luxembourg, Malta and Slovenia, are not included.

2 This is because the sample structure information can only be linked to the longitudinal dataset through household identifiers, not the cross-sectional dataset, which is limited by the particular randomization of identifiers it employs. Note as well that the longitudinal and cross-sectional components cannot be linked through household identifiers (European Commission, 2010c).

3 These regions are Åland (Finland), Limousin, Corse, Guadeloupe, Martinique, French Guiana and Réunion (France). A strategy pursued in previous studies involves aggregating data at 'higher' NUTS levels (Castells-Quintana et al, 2015), but this was not an option here since I am

specifically interested in estimating the effects of regional development funding allocated at NUTS levels 1 *and* 2, my unit of analysis.

4 The Theil index is highly correlated with the Gini coefficient (N=888; r=0.912); the squared coefficient of variation is moderately correlated with Gini (N=888; r=0.605); and Gini correlates at r=0.670 with P90/50, compared to r=0.469 with P90/10 (N=272).

5 Another good proxy for social inclusion is the long-term unemployment rate. However, since rates of unemployment and long-term unemployment are almost perfectly correlated (N=2,404, r=0.91), and the correlations between the other labour market measures employed here are moderate, ranging from c.0.592–0.674, I report the results for unemployment rates.

6 The reported differences in well-being between rich and poor regions are statistically significant at $p<0.05$, unless indicated otherwise. For the assessment, I conducted separate t-tests for each well-being indicator for each of the three EU multiannual funding periods.

7 This is seen in the correlation between Gini and Gini growth (r=0.44, N=211), whereas there was no relationship between Gini and Gini growth before the crisis (r=0.11, N=190).

Chapter Five

1 Regression analysis is well-suited to quantify associations by estimating the 'independent effects' of several explanatory factors (independent variables) on an outcome (the dependent variable) by comparatively adjudicating between the explanatory power of the independent variables.

2 Deeper lags were explored but no consistent results were found. These null findings are not reported here for the sake of brevity but are available from the author upon request.

3 The formula is $\frac{GDP_{t-2} - GDP_{t-1}}{GDP_{t-1}}$, where GDP is GDP per capita in constant prices, constant PPP million, OECD base year. Source: Eurostat.

4 While EU social investment effects are statistically significant in the main models (Appendix Tables E.1–E.3), they do not hold when addressing potential endogeneity by using a linear generalized method of moments (GMM) estimator (see Roodman, 2006, and the online appendix).

5 No consistent results for deeper lags than one and two years were found.

6 This effect size calculation is based on Model 1 in Table 5.1, which is a linear-log model. The expected change in unemployment rates (y_{ij}) associated with a $p=100\%$ increase in social funds per capita (x_{ij}) is calculated as $\beta_{EU\ social\ investments} \cdot \log([100 + p]/100)$. For region i in year j.

7 According to the 2011 Census, Scotland's workforce aged between 15 and 74 was about 4 million, which is the number used in the example for Scotland. See www.scotlandscensus.gov.uk/census-releases, accessed 25 August 2020.

8 This effect size calculation is based on Model 2 in Table 5.1, which is a log-log model. The proportional change in employment per capita (y_{ij}) associated with a *p=100%* increase in social funds per capita (x_{ij}) is calculated as a = log([100 + p]/100) and then $e^{a\beta_{EU\ social\ investments}}$. For region i in year j.

9 These null findings are not reported here for the sake of brevity but are available from the author on request.

10 Deeper lags were explored but no consistent results were found. These null findings are not reported here for the sake of brevity but are available from the author on request.

11 There are also statistically significant coefficients of EU social investments for other distributive justice measures, but they are not consistent across alternative model specifications, which variously test for omitted variable bias, endogeneity and potential time trends.

12 This effect size calculation is based on Model 2 in Table 5.3, which is a linear-log model. The expected change in Gini (y_{ij}) associated with a p=100% increase in social funds per capita (x_{ij}) is calculated as $\beta_{EU\ social\ investments}$·log([100 + p]/100). For region i in year j.

13 This effect size calculation is based on Model 4 in Table 5.3, which is a log-log model. The proportional change in the squared coefficient of variation (y_{ij}) associated with a *p=100%* increase in social funds per capita (x_{ij}) is calculated as a = log([100 + p]/100) and then $e^{a\beta_{EU\ social\ investments}}$. For region i in year j.

14 Tests using economic spending yielded null findings and are available from the author on request.

Chapter Six

1 Interview, cabinet member, DG Regio, 4 February 2010.

2 Europe Daily Bulletin, 'Dombrovskis will have his work cut out to flesh out his portfolio', Brussels: Agence Europe, 6 October 2014.

3 Europe Daily Bulletin, 'Commission wants to mobilise EFSM for €7 billion', Brussels: Agence Europe, 16 July 2015.

4 See, for example, Euractiv press release, 'Socialists, centre-right quibble over eurozone reforms', 17 March 2011; Euractiv press release, '"Calculating real recovery": what is fair growth in Europe?', 26 May 2011; Euractiv press release, 'PES Fair Growth Conference: "Transparency

is a weapon of mass destruction of privileges" says EU Commissioner Pierre Moscovici', 26 March 2015.

5 For more details about annual allocations in the period 2014–20, see Council Regulation (EU, EURATOM) No 1311/2013 of 2 December 2013 laying down the multiannual financial framework for the years 2014–20.

6 Interview, head of unit, Committee of the Regions, 10 February 2010.

7 Interview, head of unit, Ministry of Economic Affairs, Infrastructure, Transport and Technology, Munich, Germany, 17 March 2010.

8 These commitment data do not contain information about the provision of microcredit guarantees extended through the European Investment Fund or the European Progress Microfinance Facility. Data were compiled from the lists of final ERDF and ESF beneficiaries provided by regional and national authorities managing OPs (Dellmuth, 2011b).

9 The details of this analysis are elaborated on and presented in the Online Appendix S7.

10 Interviews, mayor, local government, Germany, 5 March 2010; director, chamber of commerce, Germany, 6 May 2010; MEP, Brussels, 28 January 2010; Deputy Head of Unit, DG Regio, 10 February 2010; head of department, local city hall, Ludwigshafen, Germany, 9 March 2010; consultant, German Centre for Production and Innovation, Germany, 16 June 2010; official, Wirtschaftsförderungsgesellschaft Villingen-Schwenningen, Germany, 14 May 2010; senior official, Karlsruhe Regional Council, Germany, 16 April 2010; two senior officials, chambers of commerce, Karlsruhe, Germany, 6 May 2010; senior official, Ministry of Economic Affairs, Labour and Housing Construction, Baden-Württemberg, Stuttgart, Germany, 17 June 2010.

11 Interviews, head of department, City Hall Ludwigshafen, Germany, 9 March 2010; consultant, German Centre for Production and Innovation, Rationalisierungs- und Innovationszentrum der Deutschen Wirtschaft e.V., Germany, 17 June 2010; official, Wirtschaftsförderungsgesellschaft Villingen-Schwenningen, Germany, 14 May 2010.

12 Interview, top-level civil servant, DG Regio, 4 February 2010.

13 Interviews, Director, Chamber of Commerce, Germany, 6 May 2010; Mayor, Germany, 5 March 2010; Director, Local Spatial Planning Agency, Germany, 9 March 2010; Head of Department, Local Spatial Planning Agency, Germany, 9 March 2010; Director, Regional Funding Agency, Germany, 6 May 2010.

14 Interview with head of unit, Ministry of Economic Affairs, Infrastructure, Transport and Technology, Munich, Germany, 17 March 2010.

15 See the project homepage of the ESF in Rhineland-Palatinate at https://esf.rlp.de/der-esf-in-rheinland-pfalz/organisationsstruktur/. Last accessed: 30 April 2020.

16 See, for example, Drucksachen 15/708 and 15/3364 of Landtag Rheinland-Pfalz, 15. Wahlperiode.

17 Interview, Director, Regional Funding Agency, Germany, 6 May 2010.

18 Europe Daily Bulletin, 'Rome takes control of over-indebted Sicily', Brussels: Agence Europe, 27 July 2012.

19 Interviews, senior official, City Hall Germersheim, Germany, 5 March 2010; senior official, *ifex* – initiative for start-ups and business transfer of the Ministry of Economic Affairs, Labour and Housing Construction, Baden-Württemberg, Germany, 17 June 2010.

20 Interview, head of unit, European Court of Auditors, 16 February 2010.

21 EU Observer, 'Auditor appeals for EU funds on child poverty', Brussels, 30 September 2020.

22 Interview, head of unit, European Court of Auditors, 16 February 2010.

23 Interviews, cabinet member, DG Regio, 4 February 2010; deputy head of unit, DG Regio, 10 February 2010; head of unit, Ministry of Economic Affairs, Infrastructure, Transport and Technology, Munich, Germany, 17 March 2010; head of unit, Committee of the Regions, 10 February 2010.

Chapter Seven

1 These are population figures from 2013, the final year of the observed time period. The EU member states had a combined population of 504 million people in 2013, which means that my analysis covered about 85 per cent of the total population of the EU 27.

2 For more information about the convention, see https://ec.europa.eu/social/main.jsp?langId=en&catId=1226&eventsId=1394&furtherEvents=yes, accessed 10 September 2020.

References

Acemoglu, D. (2009) *Introduction to Modern Economic Growth*, Princeton: Princeton University Press.

Acemoglu, D., Johnson, S. and Robinson, J.A. (2005) 'Institutions as a fundamental cause of long-run growth', in P. Aghion and S.N. Durlauf (eds) *Handbook of Economic Growth*, Amsterdam: Elsevier, pp. 1385–472.

Adler, M.D. and Fleurbaey, M. (eds) (2016) *The Oxford Handbook of Well-Being and Public Policy*, Oxford: Oxford University Press.

Albaek, K., Asplund, R., Barth, E., Lindahl, L., Von Simson, K. and Vanhala, P. (2015) *Youth Unemployment and Inactivity: A Comparison of School-to-Work Transitions and Labour Market Outcomes in Four Nordic Countries*, Copenhagen: Nordic Council of Ministers.

Alegre, J.G. (2012) 'An evaluation of EU regional policy. Do structural actions crowd out public spending?', *Public Choice*, 151(1–2): 1–21.

Algan, Y., Guriev, S., Papaioannou, E. and Passari, E. (2017) 'The European trust crisis and the rise of populism', *Brookings Papers on Economic Activity*, 48(2): 309–82.

Alkire, S. (2016) 'The capability approach and well-being measurement for public policy', in M.D. Adler and M. Fleurbaey (eds) *The Oxford Handbook of Well-Being and Public Policy*, Oxford: Oxford University Press, pp. 615–44.

Amin, A. and Tomaney, J. (1995) 'The challenge of cohesion', in A. Amin and J. Tomaney (eds) *Behind the Myth of European Union: Prospects for Cohesion*, London and New York: Routledge, pp. 10–47.

Aranguiz, A. (2019) 'Social mainstreaming through the European pillar of social rights: shielding 'the social' from 'the economic' in EU policymaking', *European Journal of Social Security*, 20(4): 341–63.

Atkinson, A.B. and Bourguignon, F. (2015) 'Introduction: income distribution today', in A.B. Atkinson and F. Bourguignon (eds) *Handbook of Income Distribution*, Amsterdam: Elsevier, pp. xvii–lxiv.

Atkinson, T., Cantillon, B., Marlier, E. and Nolan, B. (eds) (2002) *Social Indicators: The EU and Social Inclusion*, Oxford: Oxford University Press.

Bache, I. (1998) *The Politics of European Union Regional Policy: Multi-Level Governance or Flexible Gatekeeping*, Sheffield: Sheffield Academic Press.

Bachtler, J. and Mendez, C. (2007) 'Who governs EU cohesion policy? Deconstructing the reforms of the Structural Funds', *Journal of Common Market Studies*, 45(3): 535–64.

Bachtler, J., Wishlade, F. and Mendez, C. (2007) 'New budget, new regulations, new strategies: the 2006 reform of EU cohesion policy', European Policy Research Paper No. 63, October, Available from: www.eprc-strath.eu/public/dam/jcr:8d47d97a-2338-41b1-9dd6-c38fd50933bb/EPRP%2063.pdf [Accessed 4 August 2020].

Bachtler, J., Begg, I., Polverari, L. and Charles, D. (2013) 'Evaluation of the Main Achievements of Cohesion Policy Programmes and Projects over the Longer Term in 15 Selected Regions (from 1989–1993 Programme Period to the Present)' (2011. CE.16.B.AT.015), Final Report to the European Commission (DG Regio), European Policies Research Centre, University of Strathclyde (Glasgow) and London School of Economics.

Bachtler, J., Ferry, M. and Gal, F. (2018) *Financial Implementation of European Structural and Investment Funds*, Brussels: European Union.

Bachtler, J., Oliveira Martins, J., Wostner, P. and Zuber, P. (2019) *Towards Cohesion Policy 4.0: Structural Transformation and Inclusive Growth*, Abingdon: Routledge.

Bähr, C. (2008) 'How does sub-national autonomy affect the effectiveness of Structural Funds?', *Kyklos*, 61(1): 3–18.

Barca, F. (2009) 'An agenda for a reformed cohesion policy. A place-based approach to meeting European Union challenges and expectations', Independent Report prepared at the request of Danuta Hübner, Commissioner for Regional Policy, April, Available from: https://ec.europa.eu/regional_policy/archive/policy/future/pdf/report_barca_v0306.pdf [Accessed 4 August 2020].

Barcevicius, E., Weishaupt, T. and Zeitlin, J. (eds) (2014) *Assessing the Open Method of Coordination: Institutional Design and National Influence of EU Social Policy Coordination*, Basingstoke: Palgrave Macmillan.

Barrington-Leigh, C. and Escande, A. (2018) 'Measuring progress and well-being: a comparative review of indicators', *Social Indicators Research*, 135(3): 893–925.

Barro, R.J. and Sala-i-Martin, X. (1991) 'Convergence across states and regions', *Brookings Papers on Economic Activity*, 1: 107–82.

Bassanini, A. and Duval, R. (2006) 'Employment patterns in OECD countries: reassessing the role of policies and institutions', OECD Social, Employment, and Migration Working Papers, No. 35, 9 June, Available from: www.oecd.org/employment/emp/36888714.pdf [Accessed 4 August 2020].

Becker, S.O., Egger, P.H. and Von Ehrlich, M. (2010) 'Going NUTS: the effect of EU Structural Funds on regional performance', *Journal of Public Economics*, 94: 578–90.

Becker, S.O., Hornung, E. and Woessmann, L. (2011) 'Education and catch-up in the industrial revolution', *American Economic Journal: Macroeconomics*, 3(3): 92–126.

Becker, S.O., Egger, P.H. and Von Ehrlich, M. (2012) 'Too much of a good thing? On the growth effects of the EU's regional policy', *European Economic Review*, 56(4): 648–68.

Becker, S.O., Egger, P.H. and Von Ehrlich, M. (2013) 'Absorptive capacity and the growth and investment effects of regional transfers: a regression discontinuity design with heterogeneous treatment effects', *American Economic Journal: Economic Policy*, 5(4): 29–77.

Beckfield, J. (2006) 'European integration and income inequality', *American Sociological Review*, 71(6): 964–85.

Beckfield, J. (2019) *Unequal Europe: Regional Integration and the Rise of European Inequality*, Oxford: Oxford University Press.

Begg, I. (2003) 'Completing EMU: rethinking cohesion policy', *Oxford Review of Economic Policy*, 19(1): 161–79.

Begg, I. (2009) 'The future of cohesion policy in richer regions', *European Union Regional Policy Working Papers*, 3/2009.

Begg, I. and Bachtler, J. (2017) 'Cohesion policy after Brexit: the economic, social and institutional challenges', *Journal of Social Policy*, 46(4): 745–63.

Bertinelli, L. and Zou, B. (2008) 'Does urbanization foster human capital accumulation?', *The Journal of Developing Areas*, 41(2): 171–84.

Beugelsdijk, M. and Eijffinger, S.C.W. (2005) 'The effectiveness of structural policy in the European Union: an empirical analysis for the EU-15 in 1995–2001', *Journal of Common Market Studies*, 43(1): 37–51.

Bodenstein, T. and Kemmerling, A. (2011) 'Ripples in a rising tide: why some EU regions receive more Structural Funds than others', European Integration online Papers No. 16, Available from: http://eiop.or.at/eiop/texte/2012-001a.htm [Accessed 29 June 2019].

Boix, C. (1998) *Political Parties, Growth and Equality: Conservative and Social Democratic Economic Strategies in the World Economy*, Cambridge: Cambridge University Press.

Boldrin, M. and Canova, F. (2001) 'Inequality and convergence in Europe's regions: reconsidering European regional policies', *Economic Policy*, 16(32): 205–53.

Bondonio, D. and Greenbaum, R. (2006) 'Do business investment incentives promote employment in declining areas? Evidence from EU Objective-2 regions', *European Urban and Regional Studies*, 13: 225–44.

Bonoli, G. and Liechti, F. (2018) 'Good intentions and Matthew effects: access biases in participation in active labour market policies', *Journal of European Public Policy*, 25(6): 894–911.

Bouget, D., Frazer, H., Marlier, E. and Sabato, S. (eds) (2015) *Social Investment in Europe. A Study of National Policies*, Brussels: European Commission.

Boulant, J., Brezzi, M. and Veneri, P. (2016) 'Income levels and inequality in metropolitan areas: a comparative approach in OECD countries', OECD Regional Development Working Papers, No. 2016/06, Paris: OECD Publishing. https://doi.org/10.1787/5jlwj02zz4mr-en.

Bouvet, F. (2005) 'European Union regional policy: allocation determinants and effects on regional economic growth', Working Paper, Department of Economics, University of California, 11 February, Available from: www.ub.edu/sea2009.com/Papers/117.pdf [Accessed 29 June 2019].

Bouvet, F. (2010) 'EMU and the dynamics of regional per capita income inequality in Europe', *Journal of Economic Inequality*, 83: 23–344.

Bouvet, F. and Dall'erba, S. (2010) 'European Regional Structural Funds: how large is the influence of politics on the allocation process?', *Journal of Common Market Studies*, 48(6): 501–28.

Brazier, J.E., Harper, R., Jones, N.M., O'Cathain, A., Thomas, K.J., Usherwood, T. and Westlake, L. (1992) 'Validating the SF-36 health survey questionnaire: new outcome measure for primary care', *British Medical Journal*, 305: 160–64.

Burnside, C. and Dollar, D. (2000) 'Aid, policies and growth', *American Economic Review*, 90(4): 847–68.

Busemeyer, M.R. (2014) *Skills and Inequality: Partisan Politics and the Political Economy of Education Reforms in Western Welfare States*, Cambridge: Cambridge University Press.

Busemeyer, M.R. and Tober, T. (2015) 'European integration and the political economy of inequality', *European Union Politics*, 16(4): 536–57.

Busemeyer, M.R., de la Porte, C., Garritzmann, J.C. and Pavolini, E. (2018) 'The future of the social investment state: politics, policies, and outcomes', *Journal of European Public Policy*, 25(6): 801–9.

Cantillon, B. (2011) 'The paradox of the social investment state: growth, employment and poverty in the Lisbon era', *Journal of European Social Policy*, 21(5): 432–49.

Cappelen, A., Castellacci, F., Fagerberg, J. and Verspagen, B. (2003) 'The impact of EU regional support on growth and convergence in the European Union', *Journal of Common Market Studies*, 41(4): 621–44.

Carruthers, C.P. and Hood, C.D. (2004) 'The power of the positive: leisure and well-being', *Therapeutic Recreation Journal*, 38(2): 225–46.

Castelló-Climent, A. and Doménech, R. (2014) 'Human capital and income inequality: some facts and some puzzles', BBVA Research Working Paper 12/28.

Castells-Quintana, D., Ramos, R. and Royuela, V. (2015) 'Income inequality in European regions: recent trends and determinants', *Review of Regional Research*, 35(2): 123–46.

Chalmers, A.W. (2013) 'Regional authority, transnational lobbying and the allocation of Structural Funds in the European Union', *Journal of Common Market Studies*, 51(5): 815–31.

Charron, N. (2016) 'Explaining the allocation of regional Structural Funds: the conditional effect of governance and self-rule', *European Union Politics*, 17(4): 638–59.

Charron, N., Lapuente, V. and Rothstein, B. (2013) *Quality of Government and Corruption from a European Perspective: A Comparative Study of Good Government in EU Regions*, Cheltenham, UK: Edward Elgar.

Coelho, M. (2019) 'Fiscal stimulus in a monetary union: Evidence from Eurozone regions', *Palgrave Macmillan & International Monetary Fund IMF Economic Review* 67(3): 573–617.

Collier, P. (2018) *The Future of Capitalism: Facing the New Anxieties*, London: Penguin.

Commission of the European Communities (1994) *Sixth Annual Report on the Structural Funds, COM (95)583 final*, Commission of the European Communities, 14 December, Available from: http://aei.pitt.edu/4012/1/4012.pdf [Accessed 6 August 2020].

Commission of the European Communities (2001) *European Governance. A White Paper, COM (2001)428*, Commission of the European Communities, 25 July, Available from: https://ec.europa.eu/commission/presscorner/detail/en/DOC_01_10 [Accessed 17 March 2021].

Conzelmann, T. (1995) 'Networking and the politics of EU regional policy: lessons from North Rhine-Westphalia, Nord-Pas de Calais and North West England', *Regional and Federal Studies*, 51: 34–172.

Court of Auditors (2008) 'Annual report on the implementation of the budget, 2009/C 269/01', *Official Journal of the European Union*, 52(10 November), Available from: https://eur-lex.europa.eu/legal-content/EN/TXT/PDF/?uri=CELEX:52009TA1110(01)&from=EN [Accessed 6 August 2020].

Croezen, S., Burdorf, A. and van Lenthe, F.J. (2016) 'Self-perceived health in older Europeans: does the choice of survey matter?', *European Journal of Public Health*, 26(4): 686–92.

Cylus, J. and Pearson, M. (2015) 'The crisis and its implications for household financial security, government resources and health expenditure', in S. Thomson, J. Figueras, T. Evetovits, M. Jowett, P. Mladovsky, A. Maresso, J. Cylus, M. Karanikolos and H. Kluge (eds) *Economic Crisis, Health Systems and Health in Europe: Impact and Implications for Policy*, Maidenhead and New York: Open University Press, pp. 17–52.

Dall'erba, S. and Le Gallo, J. (2008) 'Regional convergence and the impact of European Structural Funds 1989–1999: A spatial econometric analysis', *Papers in Regional Science*, 87(2): 219–44.

De Bruin, A., Picavet, H. and Nossikov, A. (eds) (1996) *Health Interview Surveys. Towards International Harmonization of Methods and Instruments*, WHO regional publications, European series No. 58, Copenhagen: WHO Regional Office for Europe, pp. 1–161.

De la Porte, C. (2019) 'The European pillar of social rights meets the Nordic model', *European Policy Analysis for the Swedish Institute for European Policy Studies*, January, Available from: www.sieps.se/globalassets/publikationer/2019/20192epa [Accessed 4 August 2020].

De la Porte, C. and Natali, D. (2018) 'Agents of institutional change in EU policy: the social investment moment', *Journal of European Public Policy*, 25(6): 828–43.

De Looze, M.E., Huijts, T., Stevens, G.W.J.M., Torsheim, T. and Vollebergh, W.A.M. (2018) 'The happiest kids on earth. Gender equality and adolescent life satisfaction in Europe and North America', *Journal of Youth and Adolescence*, 47(5): 1073–85.

De Rynck, S. and McAleavey, P. (2001) 'The cohesion deficit in Structural Fund policy', *Journal of European Public Policy*, 8(4): 541–57.

De Wilde, P. and Zürn, M. (2012) 'Can the politicization of European integration be reversed?', *Journal of Common Market Studies*, 50(S1): 137–53.

Dellmuth, L.M. (2011a) 'The cash divide. the allocation of European Union regional grants', *Journal of European Public Policy*, 18(7): 1016–33.

Dellmuth, L.M. (2011b) 'European structural, agricultural and environmental spending in Germany: the allocation and implementation of EU resources', European Free Alliance/Greens and Stockholm University, Policy paper, February, Available from: www.diva-portal.org/smash/get/diva2:442927/FULLTEXT01.pdf [Accessed 4 August 2020].

Dellmuth, L.M. and Chalmers, A.W. (2018) 'All spending is not equal: European Union public spending, policy feedback, and citizens' support for the EU', *European Journal of Political Research*, 57: 3–23.

Dellmuth, L.M. and Schlipphak, B. (2019) 'Legitimacy beliefs towards global governance institutions: a research agenda', *Journal of European Public Policy*, 27(6): 931–43.

Dellmuth, L.M. and Stoffel, M.F. (2012) 'Distributive politics and intergovernmental transfers: the local allocation of European Union Structural Funds', *European Union Politics*, 13(3): 413–33.

Dellmuth, L.M., Schraff, D. and Stoffel, M.F. (2017) 'Distributive politics, electoral institutions, and European structural and investment funding: evidence from France and Italy', *Journal of Common Market Studies*, 55: 275–93.

Delors, J. (1989) *Report on Economic and Monetary Union in the European Community*, European Communities, 17 April, Available from: http://aei.pitt.edu/1007/1/monetary_delors.pdf [Accessed 3 May 2019].

Dettmer, B. and Sauer, T. (2018) 'Implementation of European cohesion policy at the sub-national level: evidence from beneficiary data in Eastern Germany', *Papers in Regional Science*, 98(1): 167–89.

Dijkstra, L., Poelman, H. and Rodríguez-Pose, A. (2019) 'The geography of EU discontent', *Regional Studies*, 68: 1–17.

Dong, E., Du, H. and Gardner, L. (2020) 'An interactive web-based dashboard to track COVID-19 in real time', *The Lancet*, 20(5): 533–4.

Döpke, J., Knabe, A., Lang, C. and Maschke, P. (2017) 'Multidimensional well-being and regional disparities in Europe', *Journal of Common Market Studies*, 55(5): 1026–44.

Dupont, C. (2016) *Climate Policy Integration into EU Energy Policy: Progress and Prospects*, London and New York: Routledge.

Easterlin, R.A. (1995) 'Will raising the incomes of all increase the happiness of all?', *Journal of Economic Behavior and Organization*, 27(1): 35–48.

Easton, D. (1975) 'A re-assessment of the concept of political support', *British Journal of Political Science*, 5(4): 435–57.

Ederveen, S., de Groot, L.F. and Nahuis, R. (2006) 'Fertile soil for Structural Funds? A panel data analysis of the conditional effectiveness of European cohesion policy', *Kyklos*, 59(1): 17–42.

Eger, R.J. and Maridal, J.H. (2015) 'A statistical meta-analysis of the wellbeing literature', *International Journal of Wellbeing*, 5(2): 45–74.

Esping-Andersen, G. (2002) *Why We Need a New Welfare State*, Oxford: Oxford University Press.

Esping-Andersen, G. (2007) *The Incomplete Revolution: Adapting Welfare States to Women's New Roles*, Bristol: Policy Press.

Eurofound (2018) *Social Insecurities and Resilience*, Luxembourg: Publications Office of the European Union.

European Commission (1988) *Trade Union Information Bulletin. 1992: The Social Dimension. Structural Funds. Collective Bargaining. Privatisation*, Luxembourg: Office for Official Publications of the European Communities, Available from: http://aei.pitt.edu/41285/1/A5328.pdf [Accessed 2 March 2016].

European Commission (1996) *First Report on Economic and Social Cohesion*, Luxembourg: Office for Official Publications of the European Communities, Available from: http://aei.pitt.edu/42144/1/1st_social_cohesion.pdf [Accessed 4 August 2020].

European Commission (2000) *Agenda 2000: For a Stronger and Wider Union*, Luxembourg: Office for Official Publications of the European Communities, Available from: http://aei.pitt.edu/3137/1/3137.pdf [Accessed 4 August 2020].

European Commission (2010a) 'Regional policy contributing to smart growth in Europe 2020', Communication from the Commission to the European Parliament, the Council, the European Economic and Social Committee and the Committee of the Regions, SEC(2010) 1183, Available from: https://ec.europa.eu/regional_policy/sources/docoffic/official/communic/smart_growth/comm2010_553_en.pdf [Accessed 4 August 2020].

European Commission (2010b) 'Europe 2020. A strategy for smart, sustainable and inclusive growth', European Commission: COM(2010) 2020 final, Available from: https://eur-lex.europa.eu/LexUriServ/LexUriServ.do?uri=COM:2010:2020:FIN:EN:PDF [Accessed 4 August 2020].

European Commission (2010c) *Robustness of some EU-SILC based indicators at regional level*, Luxembourg: Publications Office of the European Union, Available from: https://ec.europa.eu/eurostat/documents/3888793/5848449/KS-RA-10-020-EN.PDF/0b2b79cd-81f0-4c97-9328-373cb70bc99a [Accessed 4 August 2020].

European Commission (2010d) *Why Socio-Economic Inequalities Increase? Facts and Policy Responses in Europe*, Luxembourg: Publications Office of the European Union, Available from: https://ec.europa.eu/research/social-sciences/pdf/policy_reviews/policy-review-inequalities_en.pdf [Accessed 4 August 2020].

European Commission (2010e) 'Deutsch-Türkisches Wirtschaftszentrum Mannheim (dtw) – German-Turkish Business Centre Mannheim', European Commission – EU Regional and Urban Development – Regional policy – Projects, Available from: https://ec.europa.eu/regional_policy/en/projects/best-practices/germany/1973 [Accessed 4 August 2020].

European Commission (2011) 'Commission Staff Working Paper: Impact Assessment, SEC(2011)1141 final'.

European Commission (2014a) *The European 2020 Poverty Target: Lessons Learned and the Way Forward. Final Report*, European Commission, Available from: https://ec.europa.eu/social/BlobServlet?docId=13002&langId=en [Accessed 4 August 2020].

European Commission (2014b) *Investing in People: EU Funding for Employment and Social Inclusion. Social Europe Guide Volume* 7, Luxembourg: Publications Office of the European Union, Available from: http://ec.europa.eu/social/BlobServlet?docId=12456 [Accessed 4 August 2020].

European Council (1999) *Berlin European Council 24–25 March 1999. Presidency Conclusions*, European Parliament, Available from: http://www.europarl.europa.eu/summits/ber1_en.htm [Accessed 29 June 2019].

European Economic Advisory Group (2012) *The EEAG Report on the European Economy 2012*, CESifo, Munich, Available from: www.ifo.de/DocDL/EEAG-2012.pdf [Accessed 24 March 2021].

European Economic Advisory Group (2021) *The EEAG Report on the European Economy - Beyond the Coronavirus Crisis: Investing for a Viable Future*, CESifo, Munich, Available from: www.ifo.de/DocDL/EEAG-2021.pdf [Accessed 24 March 2021].

European Union (2008) 'EU Cohesion Policy 1988–2008: investing in Europe's future', *Inforegio Panorama*, 26(June), Available from: https://ec.europa.eu/regional_policy/sources/docgener/panorama/pdf/mag26/mag26_en.pdf [Accessed 11 June 2019].

Eurostat (2015) *Smarter, Greener, More Inclusive? Indicators to Support the Europe 2020 Strategy*, Luxembourg: Publications Office of the European Union, Available from http://ec.europa.eu/eurostat/product?code=KS-EZ-14-001&language=en [Accessed 2 May 2019].

Eurostat (2020) 'Statistics Database', European Commission, Available from: https://ec.europa.eu/eurostat/ [Accessed 15 April 2020].

Evans, A. (2005) *EU Regional Policy*, Richmond: Richmond Law and Tax.

Fagerberg, J. (1987) 'A technology gap approach to why growth rates differ', *Research Policy*, 16: 87–99.

Fagerberg, J. and Verspagen, B. (1996) 'Heading for divergence? Regional growth in Europe reconsidered', *Journal of Common Market Studies,* 34(3): 431–48.

Fagerberg, J., Verspagen, B. and Caniëls, M. (1997) 'Technology, growth and unemployment across European regions', *Regional Studies*, 31: 457–66.

Farole, T., Rodríguez-Pose, A. and Storper, M. (2011) 'Cohesion policy in the European Union: growth, geography, institutions', *Journal of Common Market Studies*, 49(5): 1089–111.

Ferrera, M. (2014) 'Solidarity in Europe after the crisis', *Constellations*, 21(2): 222–38.

Ferrera, M. (2017) 'Impatient politics and social investment: The EU as 'policy facilitator', *Journal of European Public Policy*, 24(8): 1233–51.

Ferrera, M., Matsaganis, M. and Sacchi, S. (2002) 'Open coordination against poverty: the new EU "social inclusion process"', *Journal of European Social Policy*, 12(3): 227–39.

Fitoussi, J.-P., Sen, A. and Stiglitz, J.E. (eds) (2010) *Mismeasuring Our Lives: Why GDP Doesn't Add Up*, New York: The New Press.

Flash Eurobarometer (FEB) (various years) 'Flash Eurobarometer reports', European Commission, Available from: http://ec.europa.eu/commfrontoffice/publicopinion/archives/flash_arch_en.htm [Accessed 29 June 2019].

Fleurbaey, M. and Blanchet, D. (eds) (2013) *Beyond GDP: Measuring Welfare and Assessing Sustainability*, Oxford: Oxford University Press.

Foster, C. and Frieden, J. (2017) 'Crisis of trust: socio-economic determinants of Europeans' confidence in government', *European Union Politics*, 18(4): 511–35.

Foster, J.E. (1998) 'Absolute versus relative poverty', *American Economic Review*, 88(2): 335–41.

Foster, J.E., Greer, J. and Thorbecke, E. (1984) 'A class of decomposable poverty measures', *Econometrica*, 52(3): 761–6.

Franzese, R.J. (2002) *Macroeconomic Policies of Developed Democracies*, Cambridge: Cambridge University Press.

Frick, J.R. and Krell, K. (2011) 'Einkommensmessungen in Haushaltspanelstudien für Deutschland: Ein Vergleich von EU-SILC und SOE', *AStA Wirtschafts- und Sozialstatistisches Archiv*, 5: 221–48.

Gordon, J. (1991) 'Structural Funds and the 1992 Program in the European Community', IMF Working Papers, WP/91/65.

Hafner-Burton, E. and Pollack, M. (2009) 'Mainstreaming gender in the European Union: getting the incentives right', *Comparative European Politics,* 7: 114–38.

Hameleers, M., Bos, L. and de Vreese, C.H. (2017) '"They did it": the effects of emotionalized blame attribution in populist communication', *Communication Research*, 44(6): 870–900.

Hegelund, E. and Taalbi, J. (2019) 'What determines unemployment in the long run? Band spectrum regression on ten countries 1913–2016', Unpublished paper.

Heidenreich, M. and Wunder, C. (2008) 'Patterns of regional inequality in the enlarged Europe', *European Sociological Review*, 24(1): 19–36.

Heinemann, F., Mohl, P. and Osterloh, S. (2009) 'Who's afraid of an EU tax and why? Revenue system preferences in the European Parliament', *Review of International Organizations*, 4(1): 73–99.

Heins, E. and de la Porte, C. (2014) 'A new era of European integration? Governance of labour market and social policy since the sovereign debt crisis', *Comparative European Politics*, 13: 8–28.

Helliwell, J.F. and Putnam, R.D. (2007) 'The social context of well-being', in F. Huppert, N. Baylis and B. Keverne (eds) *The Science of Well-Being*, Oxford: Oxford University Press.

Helliwell, J.F., Layard, R., Sachs, J. and De Neve, J.-E., eds. (2020) *World Happiness Report 2020*, New York: Sustainable Development Solutions Network, Available from: https://worldhappiness.report/ [Accessed 24 March 2021].

Hemerijck, A. (2013) *Changing Welfare States*, Oxford: Oxford University Press.

Hemerijck, A. (2015) 'The quiet paradigm revolution of social investment', *Social Politics*, 22(2): 242–56.

Hemerijck, A. (2017) *The Uses of Social Investment*, Oxford: Oxford University Press.

Hobolt, S.B. (2016) 'The Brexit vote: a divided nation, a divided continent', *Journal of European Public Policy*, 23(9): 1259–77.

Hooghe, L. (1996) 'Building a Europe with the regions: the changing role of the European Commission', in L. Hooghe (ed.) *Cohesion Policy and European Integration: Building Multi-Level Governance*, Oxford: Oxford University Press, pp 89–128.

Hooghe, L. and Marks, G. (2009) 'A postfunctionalist theory of European integration: from permissive consensus to constraining dissensus', *British Journal of Political Science*, 39(1): 1–23.

Hooghe, L., Marks, G., Schakel, A.H., Chapman-Osterkatz, S., Niedzwiecki, S. and Shair-Rosenfield, S. (eds) (2016) *Measuring Regional Authority. Volume I: A Postfunctionalist Theory of Governance*, Oxford: Oxford University Press.

International Monetary Fund (2021) Government Finance Statistics (GFS), Available from: www.data.imf.org/gfs [Accessed 16 March 2021].

Janský, P., Křehlík, T. and Skuhrovec, J. (2016) 'Do EU funds crowd out other public expenditures? Evidence on the additionality principle from the detailed Czech municipalities' data', *European Planning Studies*, 24(11): 2076–95.

Jenkins, S. (2009) 'Distributionally-sensitive inequality indices and the GB2 income distribution', *Review of Income and Wealth*, 55: 392–8.

Jordan, B. (2008) *Welfare and Well-Being: Social Value in Public Policy*, Bristol: Policy Press.

Kakwani, N., Son, H.H., Qureshi, S.K. and Arif, G.M. (2004) 'Pro-poor growth: concepts and measurement with country case studies', *The Pakistan Development Review*, 42(4): 417–44.

Kakwani, N., Khandker, S. and Son, H.H. (2015) 'Income inequality and social well-being', ECINEQ, Society for the Study of Income Inequality Working Paper Series, No. 380.

Karanikolos, M., Reeves, A., Stuckler, D. and McKee, M. (2015) 'The health effects of the crisis', in S. Thomson, J. Figueras, T. Evetovits, M. Jowett, P. Mladovsky, A. Maresso, J. Cylus, M. Karanikolos and H. Kluge (eds) *Economic Crisis, Health Systems and Health in Europe: Impact and Implications for Policy*, Maidenhead and New York: Open University Press, pp. 139–58.

Katic, I. and Ingram, P. (2017) 'Income inequality and subjective well-being: toward an understanding of the relationship and its mechanisms', *Business and Society*, 57(6): 1010–44.

Kemmerling, A. and Bodenstein, T. (2006) 'Partisan politics in regional redistribution. Do parties affect the distribution of EU Structural Funds across regions?', *European Union Politics*, 7(3): 373–392.

Keyes, C.L.M. and Lopez, S. (2002) 'Toward a science of mental health: positive directions in diagnosis and interventions' in C.R. Snyder and S. Lopez (eds) *Handbook of Positive Psychology*, New York: Oxford University Press, pp. 45–59.

Kim, D. and Saada, A. (2013) 'The social determinants of infant mortality and birth outcomes in Western developed nations: a cross-country systematic review', *International Journal of Environmental Research and Public Health*, 10(6): 2296–335.

Kremer, M. (2006) 'Globalization of labor markets and inequality', *Brookings Trade Forum*, 211–28.

Kuznets, S. (1955) 'Economic growth and income inequality', *American Economic Review*, 45(1): 1–28.

Lange, S. and Vollmer, S. (2017) 'The effect of economic development on population health: a review of the empirical evidence', *British Medical Bulletin*, 121(1): 47–60.

Lipps, J. and Schraff, D. (2020) 'Regional inequality and institutional trust across Europe', *European Journal of Political Research*. https://doi.org/10.1111/1475-6765.12430.

López-Bazo, E and Royuela, V. (2019) 'Citizens' perception of the Cohesion Policy and support for the European Union', *Regional Science, Policy & Practice*, 11: 733–49.

Lundberg, O. and Manderbacka, K. (1996) 'Assessing reliability of a measure of self-rated health', *Scandinavian Journal of Social Medicine*, 24(3): 218–24.

Mack, A. (2016) 'Data handling in EU-SILC', *GESIS Papers 2016/10*.

Mack, A. and Lange, B. (2015) 'Harmonization of income data in EU-SILC', *GESIS Papers 2015/18*.

Mahler, D.G. and Ramos, X. (2019) 'Equality of opportunity in four measures of well-being', *Review of Income and Wealth*, 65: S228–55.

Mann, M. and Riley, D. (2007) 'Explaining macro-regional trends in global income inequalities, 1950–2000', *Socio-Economic Review*, 5: 81–115.

Marmot, M. (2004) *The Status Syndrome: How Your Social Standing Directly Affects Your Health*, London: Bloomsbury Publishing.

Maynou, L., Saez, M., Kyriacou A. and Bacaria, J. (2016) 'The impact of Structural and Cohesion Funds on Eurozone convergence, 1990–2010', *Regional Studies*, 50(7): 1127–39.

McGillivray, M. (2005) 'Measuring non-economic well-being achievement', *Review of Income and Wealth*, 51(2): 337–64.

McGillivray, M. and Pillarisetti, J.R. (2006) 'Human well-being concepts and measures. Adjusting human well-being indices for gender disparity: insightful empirically?', in M. McGillivray and M. Clarke (eds) *Understanding Human Well-being*, Tokyo: UN University Press, pp. 169–81.

McGillivray, M. and Shorrocks, A. (2005) 'Inequality and multidimensional well-being', *Review of Income and Wealth*, 51(2): 193–9.

Mendez, C., Bachtler, J. and McMaster, I. (2019) 'Research for REGI Committee – The agenda for cohesion policy in 2019–2024: key issues for the REGI Committee', *European Parliament, Policy Department for Structural and Cohesion Policies*, July, Available from: www.europarl.europa.eu/RegData/etudes/STUD/2019/629197/IPOL_STU(2019)629197_EN.pdf [Accessed 5 August 2020].

Milio, S. (2007) 'Can administrative capacity explain differences in regional performances? Evidence from Structural Funds implementation in southern Italy', *Regional Studies*, 41(4): 429–42.

Mohl, P. (2016) *Empirical Evidence on the Macroeconomic Effects of EU Cohesion Policy*, Wiesbaden: Springer.

Mohl, P. and Hagen, T. (2011) 'Do EU Structural Funds promote regional employment? Evidence from dynamic panel data models', European Central Bank Working Paper Series, No. 1403.

Morel, N., Palier, B. and Palme, J. (eds) (2012) *Towards a Social Investment State? Ideas, Policies and Challenges*, Bristol: Policy Press.

O'Brien Cousins, S. (1997) 'Validity and reliability of self-reported health of persons aged 70 and older', *Health Care for Women International*, 18(2): 165–74.

OECD (2010) *Regional Development Policies in OECD Countries*, Paris: OECD Publishing, Available from: www.eukn.eu/fileadmin/Lib/files/EUKN/2013/regional_development_policies_in_oecd_countries.pdf [Accessed 7 August 2020].

OECD (2011) 'Report on the Gender Initiative: Gender Equality in Education, Employment and Entrepreneurship', Meeting of the OECD Council at Ministerial Level Paris, 25–26 May, Available from: www.oecd.org/education/48111145.pdf [Accessed 5 August 2020].

OECD (2014) 'Does income inequality hurt economic growth? Focus on Inequality and Growth', OECD Directorate for Employment, Labour and Social Affairs, December, Available from: www.oecd.org/social/Focus-Inequality-and-Growth-2014.pdf [Accessed 30 March 2019].

OECD (2016) *OECD Regions at a Glance 2016*, Paris: OECD Publishing, Available from: https://doi.org/10.1787/reg_glance-2016-en.

OECD (2017a) *How's Life? Measuring Well-Being*, Paris: OECD Publishing, Available from: http://dx.doi.org/10.1787/how_life-2017-en [Accessed 1 April 2019].

OECD (2017b) *Understanding the Socio-Economic Divide in Europe*, Paris: OECD Publishing, Available from: www.oecd.org/els/soc/cope-divide-europe-2017-background-report.pdf [Accessed 1 April 2019].

OECD (2018) *OECD Regions at a Glance 2018*, Paris: OECD Publishing, Available from: https://doi.org/10.1787/reg_cit_glance-2018-en [Accessed 5 August 2020].

OECD (2019), *OECD Labour Force Statistics 2019*, Paris: OECD Publishing, Available from: https://doi.org/10.1787/g2g9fb3e-en.

OECD (2020a) *How's Life? Measuring Well-Being*, Paris: OECD Publishing, Available from: https://doi.org/10.1787/9870c393-en [Accessed 16 April 2020].

OECD (2020b) *Strengthening Governance of EU Funds under Cohesion Policy: Administrative Capacity Building Roadmaps*, Paris: OECD Publishing, Available from: https://doi.org/10.1787/9b71c8d8-en [Accessed 5 August 2020].

O'Reilly, J., Froud, J., Warhurst, C., Morgan, G., Grey, C., Wood, G., Wright, M., Boyer, R., Frerichs, S., Sankari, S., Rona-Tas, A. and Le Galès, P. (2016) 'Brexit: Understanding the socio-economic origins and consequences', *Socio-Economic Review*, 14(4): 807–54.

Osberg, L. and Sharpe, A. (2002) 'An index of economic well-being for selected OECD countries', *The Review of Income and Wealth*, 48(3): 291–316.

Pes, G.N. and Porretta, P. (2015) *Microfinance, EU Structural Funds and Capacity Building for Managing Authorities: A Comparative Analysis of European Convergence Regions*, Basingstoke: Palgrave Macmillan.

Pierson, P. (1994) *Dismantling the Welfare State? Reagan, Thatcher, and the Politics of Retrenchment*, Cambridge: Cambridge University Press.

Pierson, P. (1996) 'The path to European integration: a historical institutionalist analysis', *Comparative Political Studies*, 29(2): 123–63.

Piketty, T. (2014) *Capital in the Twenty-First Century*, Cambridge, MA: Harvard University Press.

Pollack, M.A. (2003) *The Engines of European Integration: Delegation, Agency and Agenda Setting in the EU*, Oxford: Oxford University Press.

Pontusson, J. (2005) *Inequality and Prosperity: Social Europe vs. Liberal America*, Ithaca, NY: Cornell University Press.

Putnam, H. (1981) *Reason, Truth, and History*, Cambridge: Cambridge University Press.

Putnam, R.D. (1993) *Making Democracy Work: Civic Traditions in Modern Italy*, Princeton: Princeton University Press.

Raveaud, G. and Salais, R. (2001) 'Fighting against social exclusion in a European knowledge-based society: what principles of action?', in D.G. Mayes, J. Berghman and R. Salais (eds) *Social Exclusion and European Policy*, Cheltenham: Edward Elgar.

Rawls, J. (1955) 'Two concepts of rules', *Philosophical Review*, 64: 3–32.

Rawls, J. (1971) *A Theory of Justice*, Cambridge, MA: Harvard University Press.

Rawls, J. (1993) *Political Liberalism*, New York: Columbia University Press.

Rawls, J. (2001) *Justice as Fairness: A Restatement*, Cambridge, MA: Harvard University Press.

Robine, J.M., Jagger, C. and Romieu, I. (2010) 'The minimum European health module. Background documents', EHEMU Technical report 2010_4.6, June, Available from: www.eurohex.eu/pdf/Reports_2010/2010TR4.6_Health%20Module.pdf [Accessed 29 June 2019].

Rodríguez-Pose, A. (2018) 'The revenge of the places that don't matter (and what to do about it)', *Cambridge Journal of Regions, Economy and Society*, 11(1): 189–209.

Rodríguez-Pose, A. and Fratesi, U. (2004) 'Between development and social policies: the impact of European Structural Funds in Objective 1 Regions', *Regional Studies*, 38(1): 97–113.

Rodrik, D. (2018) 'Populism and the economics of globalization', *Journal of International Business Policy*, 1: 12–33.

Romer, P.M. (1994) 'The origins of endogenous growth', *Journal of Economic Perspectives*, 8(1): 3–22.

Roodman, D. (2006) 'How to do xtabond2: an introduction to "difference" and "system" GMM in Stata', Center for Global Development Working Paper No. 103.

Rothstein, B. (1998) *Just Institutions Matter: The Moral and Political Logic of the Universal Welfare State,* Cambridge: Cambridge University Press.

Rothstein, B. and Uslaner, E.M. (2005) 'Corruption and social trust', *World Politics*, 58(3): 41–72.

Rumford, C. (2000) *European Cohesion? Contradictions in EU Integration*, Basingstoke: Palgrave Macmillan.

Salverda, W., Nolan, B. and Smeeding, T.M. (2011) 'Introduction', in B. Nolan, W. Salverda and T.M. Smeeding (eds) *The Oxford Handbook of Economic Inequality*, New York: Oxford University Press.

Sampson, R.J. (2003) 'The neighborhood context of well-being', *Perspectives in Biology and Medicine*, 46(3): S53-64.

Scharpf, F.W. (2002) 'The European social model: coping with the challenges of diversity', *Journal of Common Market Studies*, 40(4): 645–70.

Scharpf, F.W. (2009) 'Legitimacy in the multilevel European polity', *European Political Science Review*, 1(2): 173–204.

Schraff, D. (2014) 'Buying turnout or rewarding loyalists? Electoral mobilization and EU Structural Funding in the German Länder', *European Union Politics*, 15(2): 277–88.

Schraff, D. (2019) 'Regional redistribution and Eurosceptic voting', *Journal of European Public Policy*, 26(1), 83–105.

Sen, A.K. (1985) *Commodities and Capabilities*, New Delhi: Oxford University Press.

Sen, A.K (1989) 'Development as capability expansion', *Journal of Development Planning*, 19: 41–58.

Sen, A.K. (1993) 'Capability and well-being', in M. Nussbaum and A. Sen (eds) *The Quality of Life*, Oxford: Clarendon Press, pp. 30–53.

Smyrl, M.E. (1997) 'Does European Community regional policy empower the regions?', *Governance*, 10: 287–309.

Son, H.H. (2010) 'Human capital development', ADB Economics Working Paper Series, No. 225.

Son, H.H. (2011) *Equity and Well-Being: Measurement and Policy Practice*, London: Routledge.

Stewart, K. (2005) 'Dimensions of well-being in EU-regions: do GDP and unemployment tell us all we need to know?', *Social Indicators Research*, 73(2): 221–46.

Stiglitz, J.E, Fitoussi, J.P. and Durand, M. (2018) *Beyond GDP: Measuring What Counts for Economic and Social Performance*, Paris: OECD Publishing, Available from: https://read.oecd-ilibrary.org/economics/beyond-gdp_9789264307292-en#page3 [Accessed 26 June 2019].

Stockhammer, E., Guschanski, A. and Köhler, K. (2014) 'Unemployment, capital accumulation and labour market institutions in the Great Recession?', *European Journal of Economics and Economic Policies: Intervention*, 11(2): 182–94.

Sumner, L.W. (1996) *Welfare, Happiness, and Ethics*, Oxford: Clarendon Press.

Sutcliffe, J.B. (2000) 'The 1999 reform of the structural fund regulations: multi-level governance or renationalization?', *Journal of European Public Policy*, 7(2): 290–309.

Tallberg, J., Bäckstrand, K. and Scholte, J.A. (eds) (2018) *Legitimacy in Global Governance: Sources, Processes, and Consequences*, Oxford: Oxford University Press.

Thomson, S., Foubister, T. and Mossialos, E. (2009) 'Financing healthcare in the European Union: Challenges and policy responses', Observatory Studies Series, 17, Copenhagen: World Health Organization.

Tödtling-Schönhofer, H., Hamza, C., Radzyner, A., Bachtler, J., Kah, S. and Mendez, C. (2014) *Implementation of Cohesion Policy 2014–2020: Preparations and Administrative Capacity of Member States*, Brussels: European Union.

Tooze, A. (2018) *Crashed: How a Decade of Financial Crises Changed the World*, New York: Penguin Random House.

Tosun, J. (2013) 'Absorption of regional funds: a comparative analysis', *Journal of Common Market Studies*, 52(2): 371–87.

Uglanova, E.A. (2014) 'Gender dimensions of subjective well-being in Russia', in E. Eckermann (ed.) *Gender, Lifespan and Quality of Life*, Dordrecht, Netherlands: Springer, pp. 135–55.

Vandenbroucke, F., Hemerijck, A. and Palier, B. (2011) 'The EU needs a social investment pact', OSE Paper Series, Opinion paper 5.

Venkatasubramanian, V., Luoa, Y. and Sethuraman, J. (2015) 'How much inequality in income is fair? A microeconomic game theoretic perspective', *Physica A: Statistical Mechanics and its Applications*, 435: 120–38.

Verma, V., Betti, G., Natilli, M. and Lemmi, A. (2006) 'Indicators of social exclusion and poverty in Europe's regions', Working Paper No. 59, University of Siena, Department of Quantitative Methods.

Wamsler, C. (2015) 'Mainstreaming ecosystem-based adaptation: transformation toward sustainability in urban governance and planning', *Ecology and Society*, 20(2): 30.

World Bank Institute (2014) 'Introduction to poverty analysis', World Bank Group, Report No. 90288, Available from: http://documents.worldbank.org/curated/en/775871468331250546/Introduction-to-poverty-analysis [Accessed 15 July 2019].

World Development Indicators (2020) 'DataBank', Available from: https://databank.worldbank.org/source/world-development-indicators [Accessed 8 August 2020].

World Health Organization (2018) 'Making the economic case for investing in health systems. What is the evidence that health systems advance economic and fiscal objectives?', Available from: www.euro.who.int/__data/assets/pdf_file/0010/380728/pb-tallinn-01-eng.pdf?ua=1 [Accessed 20 August 2020].

Young, I.M. (2011) *Responsibility for Justice*, Oxford: Oxford University Press.

Index

S

T

U

V

W

Y

Printed and bound by CPI Group (UK) Ltd, Croydon, CR0 4YY

18/09/2026

14965016-0001